2021

ICAEW

Business Planni

TP06-34220-062

First edition 2013, Ninth edition 2020

ISBN 9781 5097 3417 7

British Library Cataloguing-in-Publication Data
A catalogue record for this book is available from the British Library

Published by

BPP Learning Media Ltd
BPP House, Aldine Place
142–144 Uxbridge Road
London W12 8AA

www.bpp.com/learningmedia

Printed in the United Kingdom

Your learning materials, published by BPP Learning Media Ltd, are printed on paper obtained from traceable sustainable sources.

The content of this publication is intended to prepare students for the ICAEW examinations, and should not be used as professional advice. Although every effort has been made to ensure that the contents of this book are correct at the time of going to press, BPP Learning Media makes no warranty that the information in this book is accurate or complete and accepts no liability for any loss or damage suffered by any person acting or refraining from acting as a result of the material in this book.

ICAEW takes no responsibility for the content of any supplemental training materials supplied by the Partner in Learning.

Welcome to BPP Learning Media's **Passcards** for ICAEW **Business Planning: Taxation.**

- They **save you time**. Important topics are summarised for you.
- They incorporate **diagrams** to kick start your memory.
- They follow the overall **structure** of the ICAEW Study Manuals, but BPP Learning Media's ICAEW **Passcards** are not just a condensed book. Each card has been separately designed for clear presentation. Topics are self contained and can be grasped visually.
- ICAEW **Passcards** are **just the right size** for pockets, briefcases and bags.
- ICAEW **Passcards focus on the exams** you will be facing.

Run through the **Passcards** as often as you can during your final revision period. The day before the exam, try to go through the **Passcards** again! You will then be well on your way to passing your exams.

Good luck!

Taxation

1: Ethics

Topic List

Your advice in relation to transactions must comply with the law and the ICAEW Code of Ethics.

You must apply scepticism and ethical judgement to a given scenario to determine the true facts and make reasoned suggestions for actions to take in relation to a given ethical dilemma.

You must be able to apply the ICAEW Code of Ethics, the Professional Conduct in Relation to Taxation, and/or anti-money laundering rules to a scenario to reach a reasoned solution.

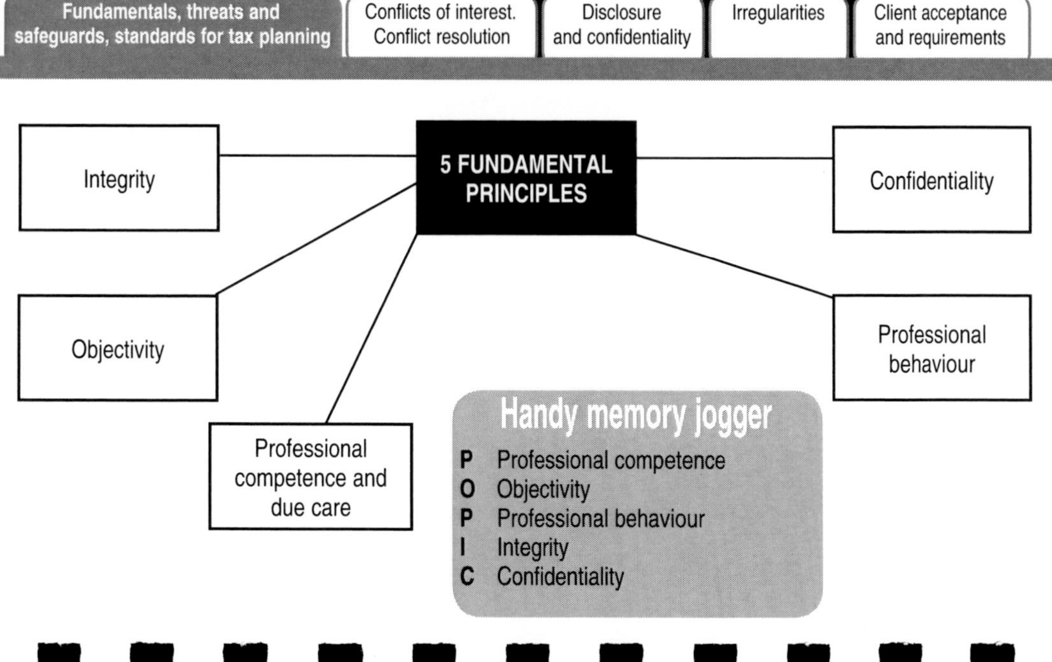
5 FUNDAMENTAL PRINCIPLES
Integrity
Confidentiality
Objectivity
Professional behaviour
Professional competence and due care
Handy memory jogger
P Professional competence
O Objectivity
P Professional behaviour
I Integrity
C Confidentiality

Threats and safeguards framework

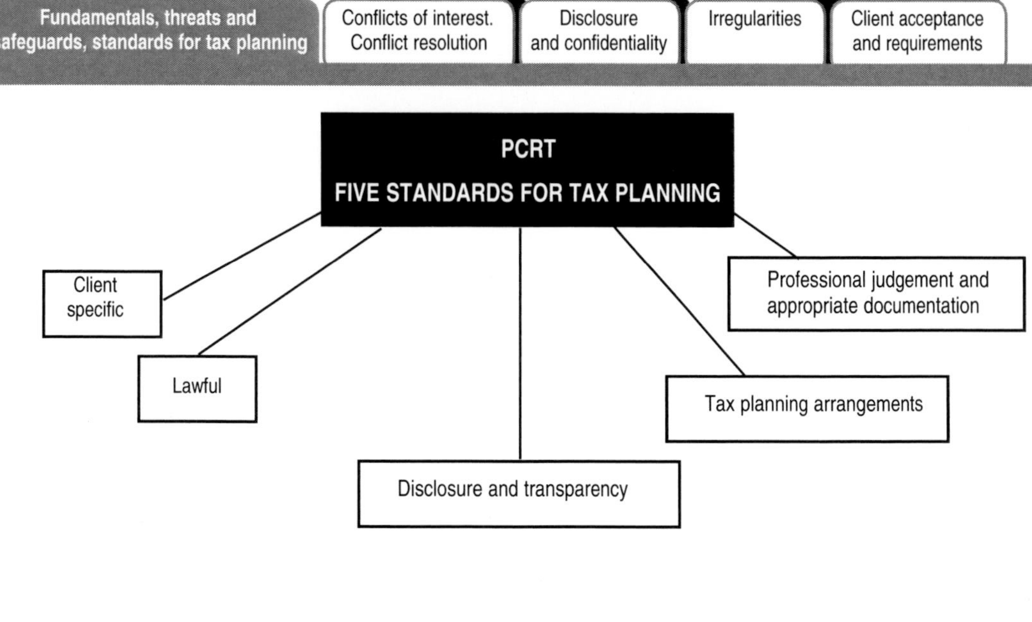
PCRT
FIVE STANDARDS FOR TAX PLANNING
Client specific
Lawful
Disclosure and transparency
Tax planning arrangements
Professional judgement and appropriate documentation

Should take reasonable steps to identify circumstances that could pose a conflict of interest.

Conflict situations

Where a firm acts for both:

- Financial involvements between client and firm (eg, loan)
- Husband and wife in a divorce settlement
- A company and its directors in their personal capacity
- Partnership and partners in their personal capacity
- Two competing businesses

Consider:

- Separate engagement teams
- Clear guidelines for teams
- Confidentiality agreements
- Regular reviews

Safeguards

- Notify the client of the conflict of interest
- Notify all parties that acting for two or more parties in a conflict matter
- Notify the client that not acting exclusively for any one client
- Obtain consent of the relevant parties to act

Alert! Do not act if one of the five fundamental principles is unacceptably threatened.

Resolving an ethical conflict

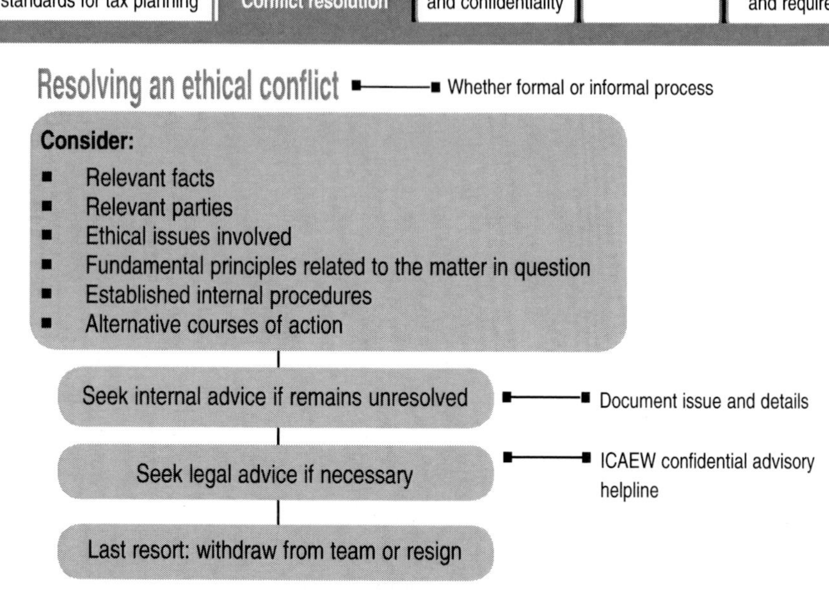

Allowed to disclose confidential information:

1 When **authorised** by the client or employer

2 When **required by law** to do so:

- Production of documents for legal proceedings
- Disclosure to the appropriate public authorities eg, under anti-money laundering legislation

3 When there is a **professional duty** or right to do so

Consider

- Will disclosure harm any interested party's interests?
- Is all known information correct?
- Is type of communication and recipient appropriate?
- Is information privileged?
- What are the legal and regulatory obligations and the possible implications of disclosure?

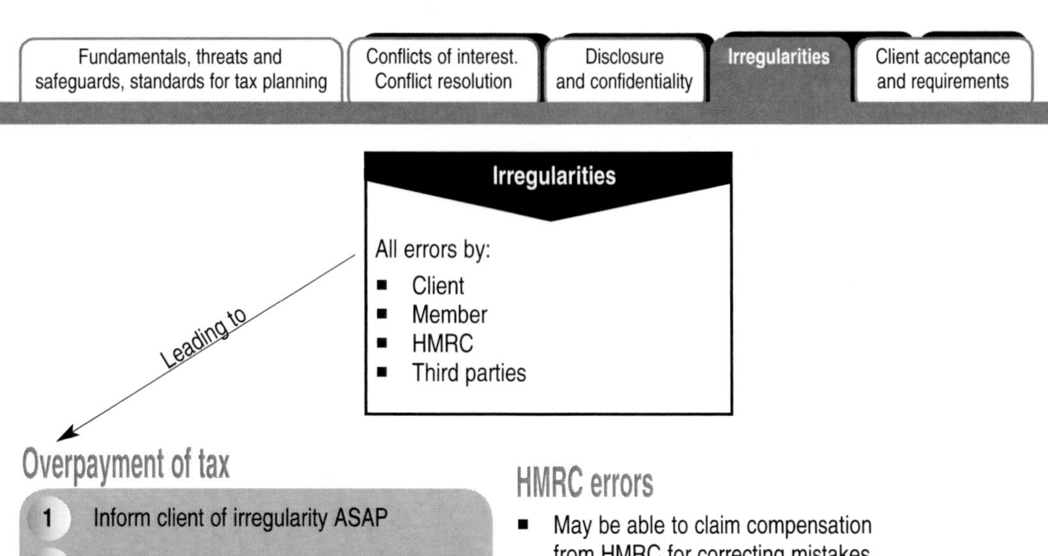

Overpayment of tax

1. Inform client of irregularity ASAP
2. Advise on making repayment claim
3. Consider time limits

HMRC errors

- May be able to claim compensation from HMRC for correcting mistakes
- Consider money laundering issues
- May need to notify PII insurers See below

Engagement letter

Contractual relationship – detailing responsibilities of:

- Client; and
- Professional accountant.

Authority to disclose for inclusion in the engagement letter:

- HMRC error
- Disclosure required by law
- Professional right or duty to disclose

Responsibility for tax returns

Client responsible for accuracy and completeness of the return

- Accountant to obtain client's written approval of the return
- May advise fuller disclosure if significant tax planning or doubt
- Accountant may sign the return on behalf of the client in certain circumstances

Professional indemnity insurance

- Required if ICAEW qualified member in public practice
- Minimum requirement:
  - Gross fee income < £600,000
    - 2½ times gross fee income
    - Minimum £100,000
  - Otherwise minimum = £1.5 million
- Cover
  - Must remain in place for at least two years after ceases public practice
  - Six years is recommended

Data protection

- Notify Information Commissioner's Office (ICO) who monitors compliance with GDPR
- Criminal offence if fail to notify

Duties of SAOs

If company has:

- Turnover > £200 million and/or
- Balance sheet > £2 billion

- SAO must certify annually that accounting systems are adequate for accurate tax reporting
- Failure = criminal offence

Anti-money laundering

Attempt to conceal the true origin or ownership of the proceeds of criminal activity or terrorist funding ('criminal property') – including the proceeds of tax evasion, benefits obtained through bribery and benefits arising from non-compliance with regulatory requirements.

Must register with an appropriate anti-money laundering supervisory authority.

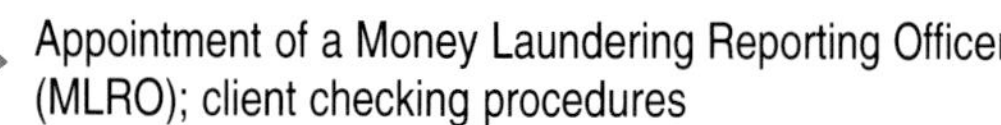

1. Client checking, record keeping and internal suspicion reporting → Appointment of a Money Laundering Reporting Officer (MLRO); client checking procedures
2. Not doing or discussing anything that might prejudice an investigation → No word or action that might 'tip off' the money launderers that they are (or may come) under investigation
3. Report suspicions (on reasonable grounds) of money laundering → Report to:
   - The Money Laundering Reporting Officer
   - National Crime Agency (use suspicious activity report (SAR))

Watch client confidentiality

Penalties: Offences tried in Magistrates' Court or Crown Court – unlimited fines and imprisonment possible

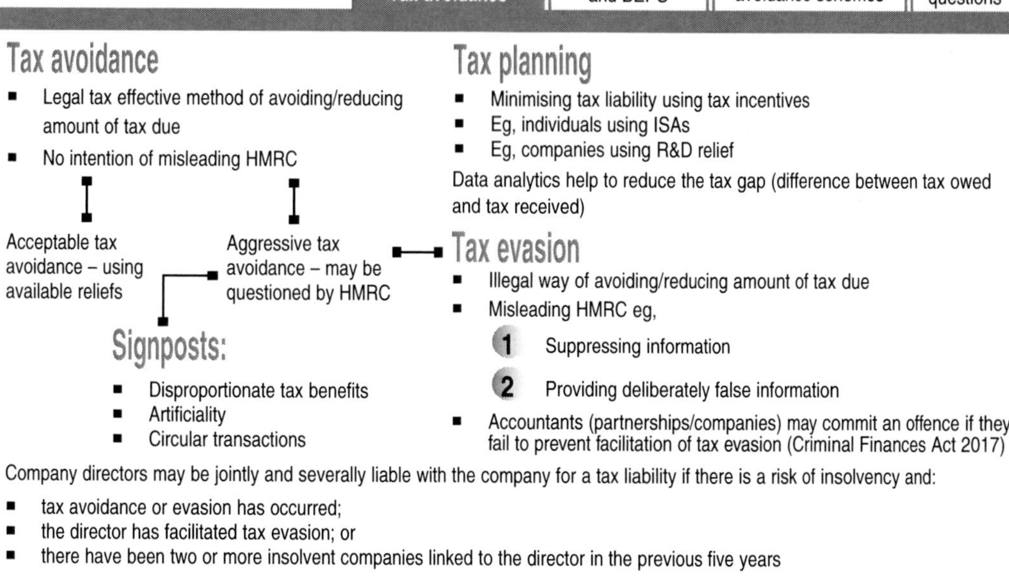

Tax avoidance

- Legal tax effective method of avoiding/reducing amount of tax due
- No intention of misleading HMRC

Acceptable tax avoidance – using available reliefs

Aggressive tax avoidance – may be questioned by HMRC

Signposts:

- Disproportionate tax benefits
- Artificiality
- Circular transactions

Tax planning

- Minimising tax liability using tax incentives
- Eg, individuals using ISAs
- Eg, companies using R&D relief

Data analytics help to reduce the tax gap (difference between tax owed and tax received)

Tax evasion

- Illegal way of avoiding/reducing amount of tax due
- Misleading HMRC eg,
  1. Suppressing information
  2. Providing deliberately false information
- Accountants (partnerships/companies) may commit an offence if they fail to prevent facilitation of tax evasion (Criminal Finances Act 2017)

Company directors may be jointly and severally liable with the company for a tax liability if there is a risk of insolvency and:

- tax avoidance or evasion has occurred;
- the director has facilitated tax evasion; or
- there have been two or more insolvent companies linked to the director in the previous five years

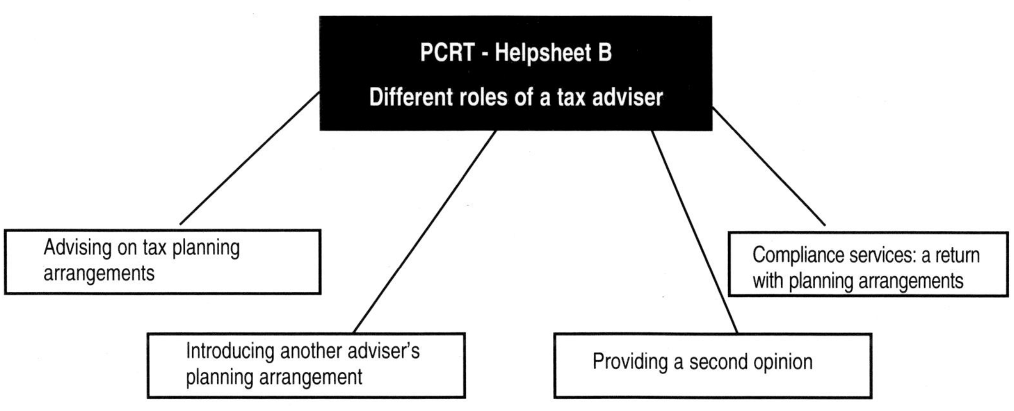
PCRT - Helpsheet B
Different roles of a tax adviser
Advising on tax planning arrangements
Introducing another adviser's planning arrangement
Providing a second opinion
Compliance services: a return with planning arrangements

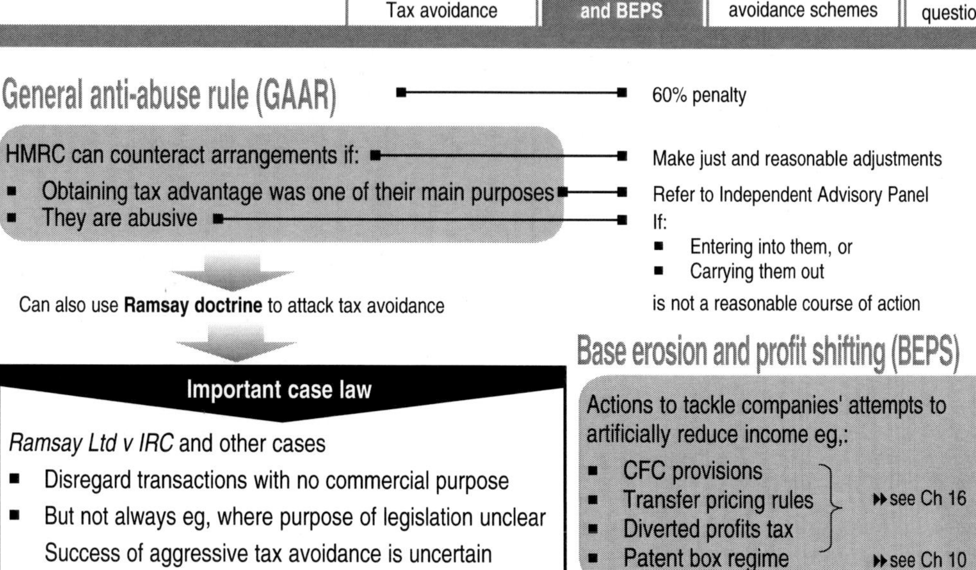

General anti-abuse rule (GAAR)
60% penalty
HMRC can counteract arrangements if:
■ Obtaining tax advantage was one of their main purposes
■ They are abusive
Make just and reasonable adjustments
Refer to Independent Advisory Panel
If:
■ Entering into them, or
■ Carrying them out
is not a reasonable course of action
Can also use Ramsay doctrine to attack tax avoidance
Important case law
Ramsay Ltd v IRC and other cases
■ Disregard transactions with no commercial purpose
■ But not always eg, where purpose of legislation unclear
Success of aggressive tax avoidance is uncertain
Base erosion and profit shifting (BEPS)
Actions to tackle companies' attempts to artificially reduce income eg,:
■ CFC provisions
■ Transfer pricing rules
■ Diverted profits tax
see Ch 16
■ Patent box regime
see Ch 10

DOTAS & DASVOIT schemes

Notify HMRC where:

- Person obtains/might obtain tax advantage
- Main/one of the main benefits of the arrangement
- Notify HMRC if scheme falls within at least 1 **hallmark**
- May have to pay tax up-front (accelerated payment)

Hallmarks

- Confidentiality
- Premium fee
- Standardised tax products
- Others specific to DOTAS
- Others specific to DASVOIT

- Promoter must notify HMRC within five days of making scheme available and for DASVOIT within 30 days of VAT being different due to the scheme
  - Promoter = responsible for design, management, marketing etc
  - May receive a conduct notice if triggers a threshold condition
- Register with HMRC
  - Unless has reasonable excuse
- Penalties for failure to comply:
  - Disclosure penalty
  - Information penalty
  - User penalty
    - Failure to report scheme reference number (SRN)

Alert! Information provided to HMRC regarding breach of DOTAS or DASVOIT rules does not breach duty of confidentiality

Ethics in the Business Planning: Taxation exam

- Embedded in scenario
- Apply knowledge to scenario
- May be expected to challenge information provided (ie, professional scepticism)
- Identify:
  - Relationship with client
  - Source of information
  - Issues

2: Income tax and NIC

Topic List

This chapter reviews certain NIC and income tax topics covered in the Tax Compliance exam.

Some traders make payments of patent royalties net of basic rate tax, which have an impact on how the tax liability is calculated.

It then deals with Individual Savings Accounts (ISAs) which allow all taxpayers, whatever their risk profile, to invest in tax free investments.

We then cover the rules for the various venture capital schemes, which aim to attract investors who are not averse to taking risks with their investments in return for valuable tax breaks.

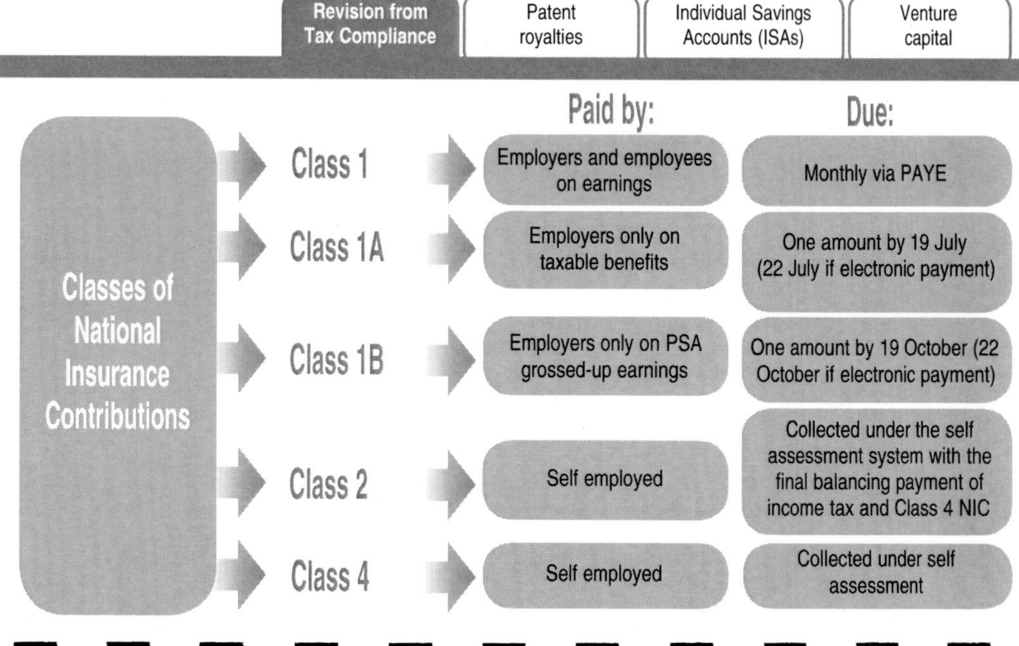
Paid by:
Due:
Classes of National Insurance Contributions
Class 1
Employers and employees on earnings
Monthly via PAYE
Class 1A
Employers only on taxable benefits
One amount by 19 July (22 July if electronic payment)
Class 1B
Employers only on PSA grossed-up earnings
One amount by 19 October (22 October if electronic payment)
Class 2
Self employed
Collected under the self assessment system with the final balancing payment of income tax and Class 4 NIC
Class 4
Self employed
Collected under self assessment

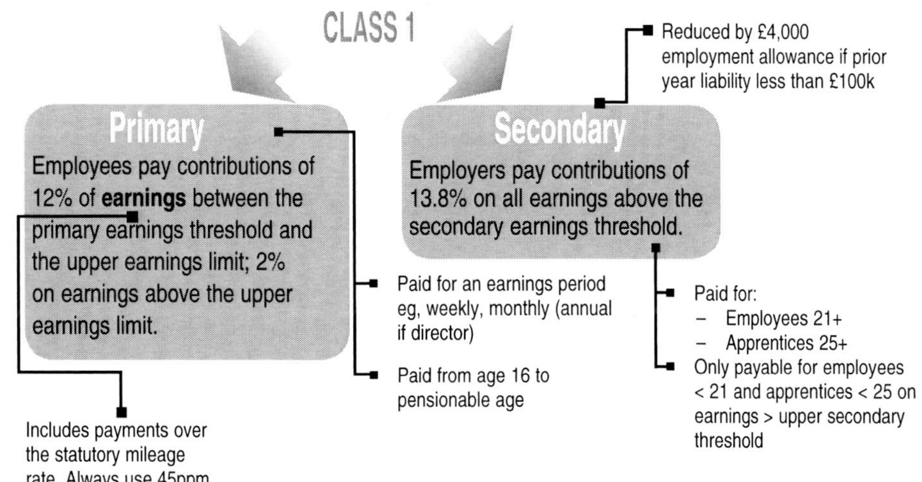
CLASS 1
Primary
Employees pay contributions of 12% of **earnings** between the primary earnings threshold and the upper earnings limit; 2% on earnings above the upper earnings limit.
Includes payments over the statutory mileage rate. Always use 45ppm
Paid for an earnings period eg, weekly, monthly (annual if director)
Paid from age 16 to pensionable age
Secondary
Employers pay contributions of 13.8% on all earnings above the secondary earnings threshold.
Reduced by £4,000 employment allowance if prior year liability less than £100k
Paid for:
– Employees 21+
– Apprentices 25+
Only payable for employees < 21 and apprentices < 25 on earnings > upper secondary threshold

CLASS 1A

Employers pay Class 1A contributions at 13.8% on most **taxable benefits** provided to their employees.

CLASS 1B

Payable by employers at 13.8% on the grossed-up value of earnings included in a **PAYE settlement agreement (PSA)**.

The self employed (ie, sole traders and partners) pay Class 2 **and** Class 4 NICs.

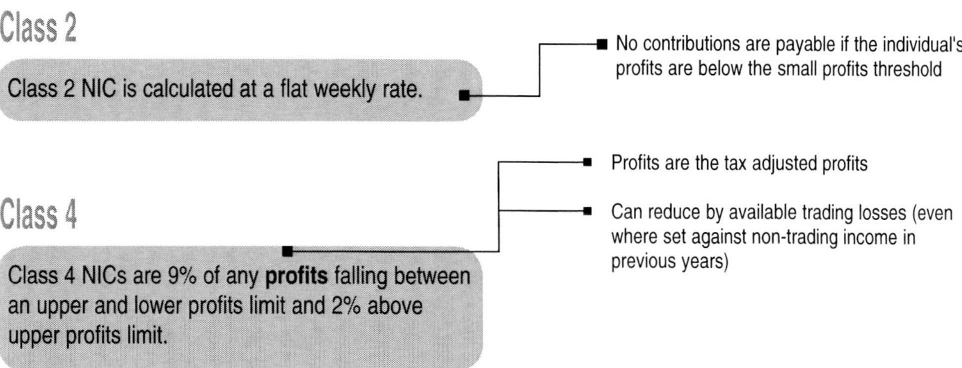

Class 2

Class 2 NIC is calculated at a flat weekly rate.

- No contributions are payable if the individual's profits are below the small profits threshold

Class 4

Class 4 NICs are 9% of any **profits** falling between an upper and lower profits limit and 2% above upper profits limit.

- Profits are the tax adjusted profits
- Can reduce by available trading losses (even where set against non-trading income in previous years)

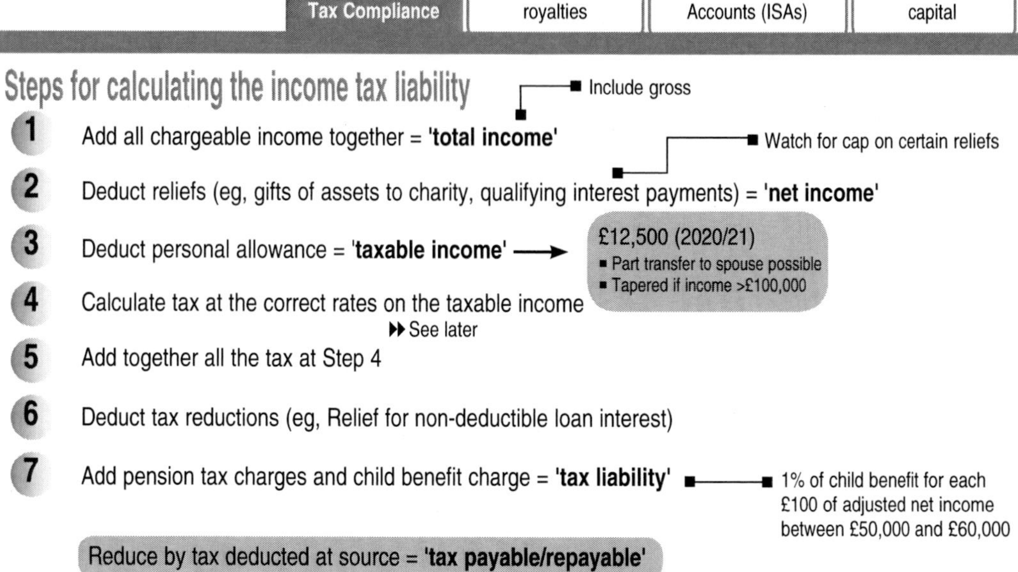
Steps for calculating the income tax liability
Include gross
1 Add all chargeable income together = 'total income'
Watch for cap on certain reliefs
2 Deduct reliefs (eg, gifts of assets to charity, qualifying interest payments) = 'net income'
3 Deduct personal allowance = 'taxable income'
£12,500 (2020/21)
Part transfer to spouse possible
Tapered if income >£100,000
4 Calculate tax at the correct rates on the taxable income
See later
5 Add together all the tax at Step 4
6 Deduct tax reductions (eg, Relief for non-deductible loan interest)
7 Add pension tax charges and child benefit charge = 'tax liability'
1% of child benefit for each £100 of adjusted net income between £50,000 and £60,000
Reduce by tax deducted at source = 'tax payable/repayable'

Tax rates

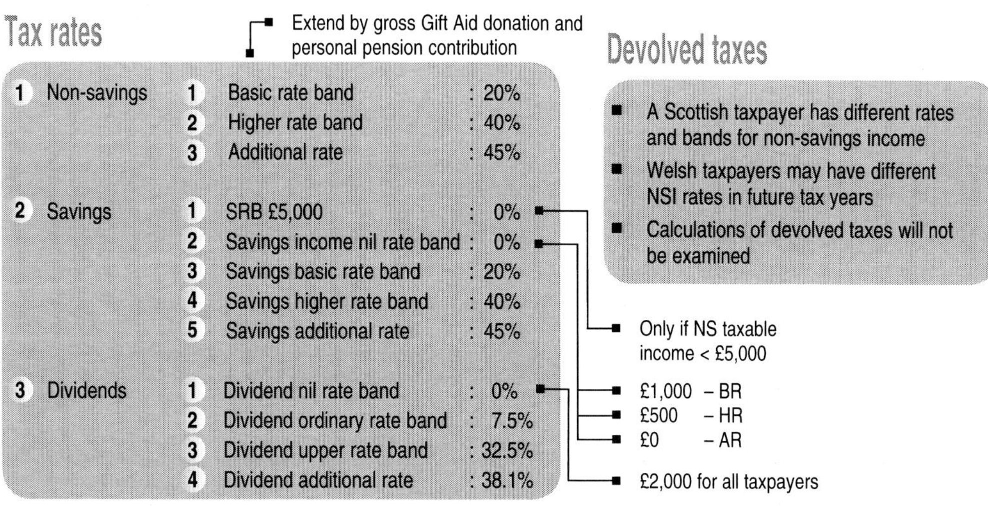

Devolved taxes

- A Scottish taxpayer has different rates and bands for non-savings income
- Welsh taxpayers may have different NSI rates in future tax years
- Calculations of devolved taxes will not be examined

Exempt income

- Interest on NS&I certificates
- Income arising on ISAs
- Betting and lottery winnings
- Premium bond winnings
- Certain social security benefits
- First £7,500 of rent under rent a room scheme
- Scholarships
- Income tax repayment interest
- Dividends on shares in a VCT
- Payments under Compensation schemes e.g. Windrush Compensation Scheme
- Apprenticeship bursary paid to care leavers.

Leave exempt income out of personal tax computations but state exempt

Apprenticeship levy

- For employers with pay bill > £3 million
- 0.5% annual pay bill
- Payable monthly

Patent royalties

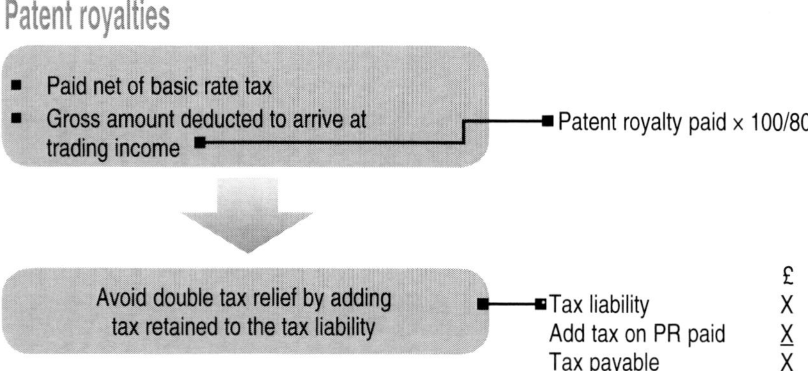

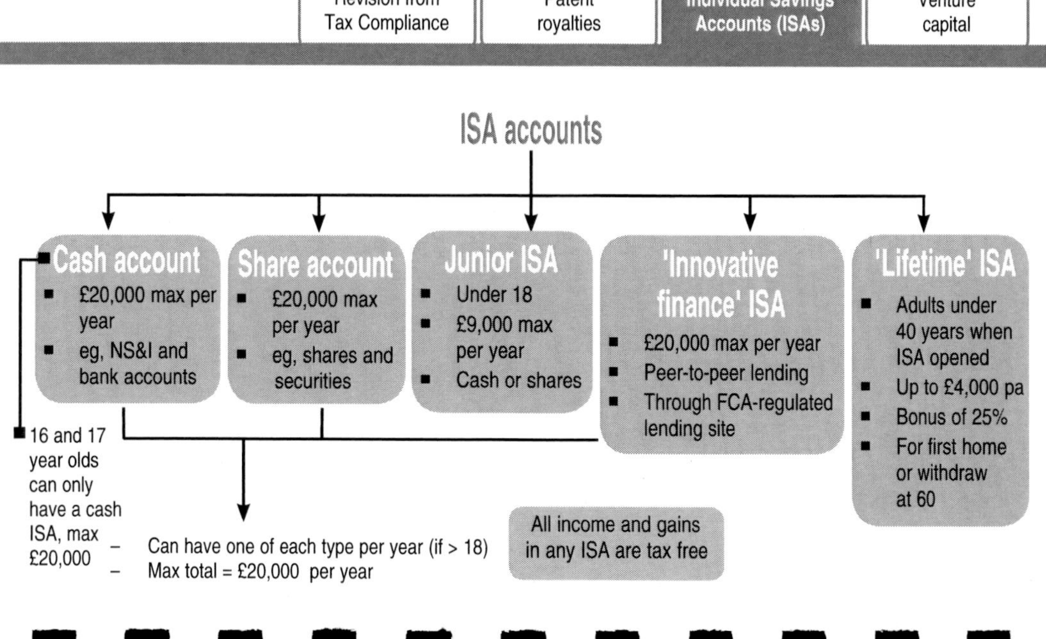
ISA accounts
Cash account
£20,000 max per year
eg, NS&I and bank accounts
Share account
£20,000 max per year
eg, shares and securities
Junior ISA
Under 18
£9,000 max per year
Cash or shares
'Innovative finance' ISA
£20,000 max per year
Peer-to-peer lending
Through FCA-regulated lending site
'Lifetime' ISA
Adults under 40 years when ISA opened
Up to £4,000 pa
Bonus of 25%
For first home or withdraw at 60
16 and 17 year olds can only have a cash ISA, max £20,000
– Can have one of each type per year (if > 18)
– Max total = £20,000 per year
All income and gains in any ISA are tax free

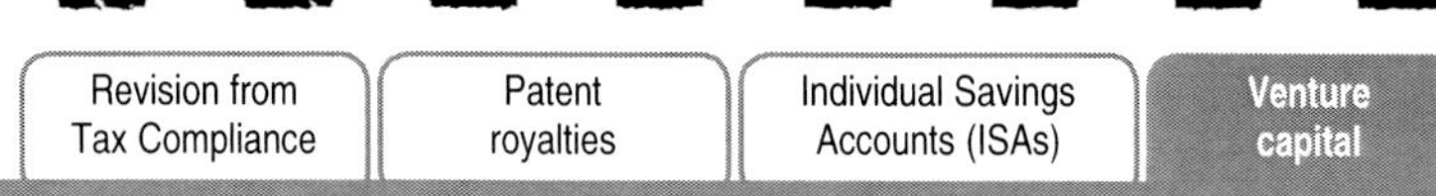

Enterprise Investment Scheme (EIS)

Investments subscribed for in the ordinary shares of unlisted trading companies, carrying on a qualifying trade, provide a tax reduction, saving income tax of 30% × investment

If the shares are not retained for at least three years the tax reduction is wholly or partly withdrawn

Max investment = £1 million a year or £2 million if investing in KICs

Knowledge Intensive Companies

Reduction given in the tax year of investment or previous year

Note: Gains made more than three years after the share issue are usually exempt from CGT

Qualifying company

- Carry on qualifying trade (no financial, asset-backed or renewable energy generation trades)
- Permanent establishment in the UK
- Unquoted
- Assets ≤ £15 million before and ≤ £16 million after issue
- < 250 full-time equivalent employees (< 500 for knowledge-intensive companies)
- ≤ £5m raised in previous 12 months, or £10m for KICs
- < £12m raised in total under EIS/VCT schemes (< £20m if knowledge-intensive company)
- Raised monies within 7yrs of 1st commercial sale (10 yrs if knowledge-intensive)
- Not in financial difficulty

Investor

Must not be connected with the company ie, must not:

- Be an employee (or non-qualifying director) or
- Own > 30% of ordinary shares/voting rights
- Hold other shares in the company — Unless founder shares or from a risk finance investment

EIS deferral relief

A gain realised by an individual on any asset can be deferred when the individual subscribes for new (ordinary shares) in an EIS company in the period commencing one year before and ending three years after the disposal.

- The shares do not need to attract EIS income tax relief.
- A qualifying company is an unquoted company carrying on a qualifying trade.
- The gain is 'frozen' and becomes chargeable if the shares are sold at any time or if certain events happen (eg, taxpayer ceases to be UK resident within the three years following issue of shares).
- A **claim** may be for any specified amount of the gain, up to the cost of the shares.

The investor can be connected with the EIS company (eg, own >30% of the shares)

Business asset disposal relief available if would have been available for original disposal

Can make use of available capital losses and annual exempt amount

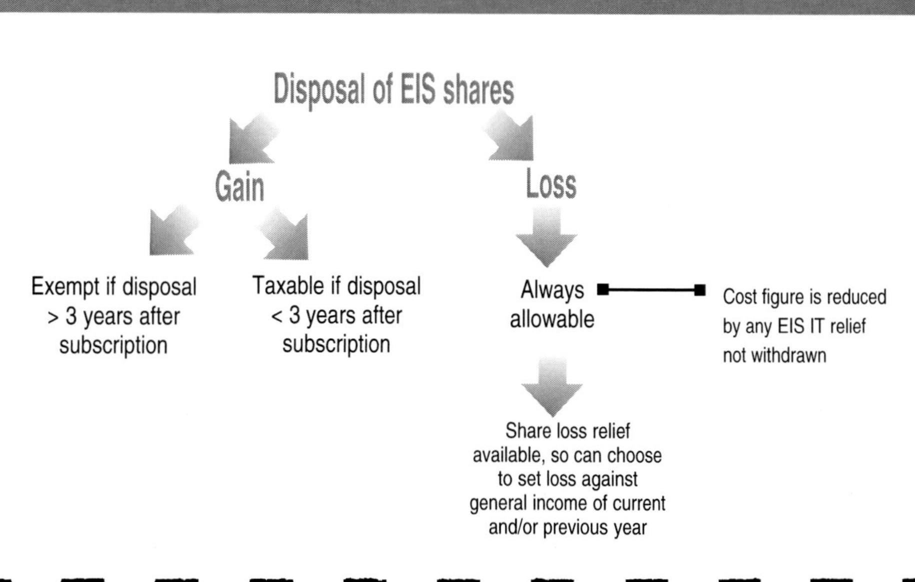
Disposal of EIS shares
Gain
Loss
Exempt if disposal > 3 years after subscription
Taxable if disposal < 3 years after subscription
Always allowable
Cost figure is reduced by any EIS IT relief not withdrawn
Share loss relief available, so can choose to set loss against general income of current and/or previous year

Seed Enterprise Investment Scheme (SEIS)

Similar to EIS scheme for smaller, early stage companies

Tax reduction of 50% × investment

Max investment = £100,000 a year

Reduction given in the tax year of investment or previous year

If the shares are not retained for at least three years the tax reduction is wholly or partly withdrawn

Note:

- Gains made > 3 years after the share issue are usually exempt from CGT
- Additional CGT exemption for gains reinvested in SEIS shares ⏩see later

Qualifying company

- Carry on new qualifying trade (as for EIS)
- Permanent establishment in the UK
- Unquoted
- Assets ≤ £200,000
- < 25 full-time equivalent employees
- Can only raise up to a lifetime maximum of £150,000
- Not in financial difficulty

Investor

Must not be connected with the company ie, must not:

- Be an employee (although can be a director), or
- Own > 30% of ordinary shares/voting rights

Same reliefs as EIS

- Disposal of SEIS shares
  - Gain exempt if held > 3 years
  - Loss allowable (but cost reduced for any remaining IT relief)
- Share loss relief available

SEIS reinvestment relief

- Gain realised on any asset may be fully or partly exempt if reinvested in SEIS shares in the same year
- Max reinvestment relief = 50% × investment
  - Max £100,000 investment
- Can only carry back reinvestment relief to previous year if also make a carry back claim for IT purposes
- Cannot also claim EIS CGT deferral in respect of same investment
- If IT relief withdrawn, reinvestment relief withdrawn to same extent

Main differences between EIS and SEIS

	EIS	SEIS
Individual		
Investment limit	up to £2 million	£100,000
IT relief	30%	50%
Director investors?	Reasonably paid only	Yes
Reinvestment relief	Deferral	Exemption (max £50,000)
Company		
Max raised investment	£5,000,000 per year	£150,000 total
Gross assets	≤ £15,000,000	≤ £200,000
Employees	< 250/< 500	< 25
Funds used in	Qualifying trade	New qualifying trade

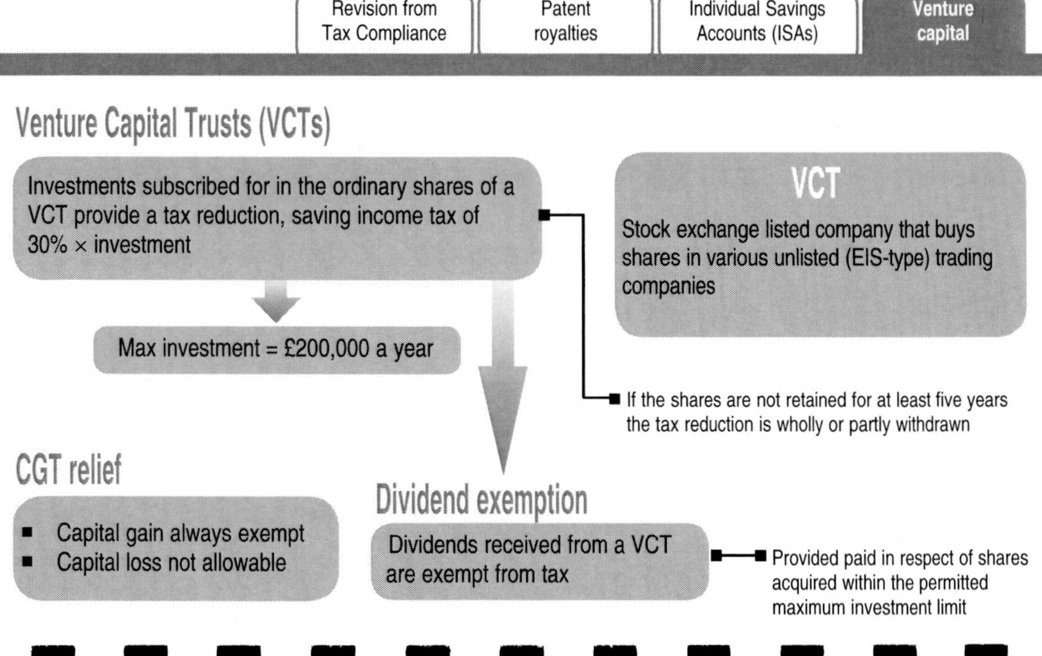
Venture Capital Trusts (VCTs)
Investments subscribed for in the ordinary shares of a VCT provide a tax reduction, saving income tax of 30% × investment
Max investment = £200,000 a year
If the shares are not retained for at least five years the tax reduction is wholly or partly withdrawn
VCT
Stock exchange listed company that buys shares in various unlisted (EIS-type) trading companies
CGT relief
Capital gain always exempt
Capital loss not allowable
Dividend exemption
Dividends received from a VCT are exempt from tax
Provided paid in respect of shares acquired within the permitted maximum investment limit

3: Employee remuneration

Topic List

- Taxable and exempt benefits
- Termination payments
- Share schemes
- Pension schemes

You need to be able to advise on the tax implications of different remuneration packages as well as appropriate structures for termination packages.

You also need to be able to advise on the appropriateness of different share schemes for a given scenario.

Non-cash benefits

- General rule = cost to employer
- Use if no specific rule

Living expenses

Living expenses connected with accommodation (eg, gas bills) are taxable. However, if the accommodation is job-related, the maximum amount taxable is 10% × net earnings.

Accommodation

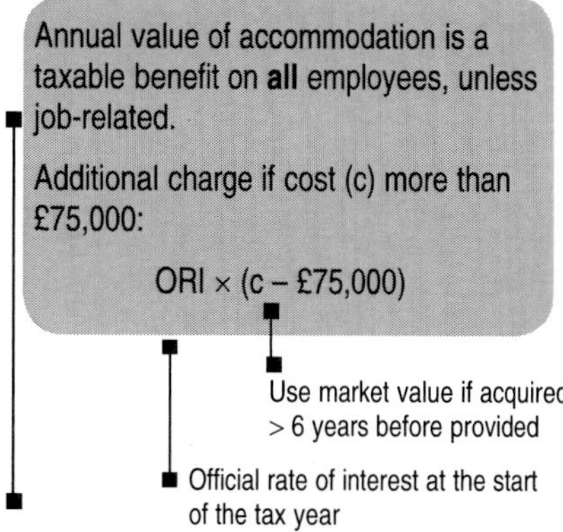

Annual value of accommodation is a taxable benefit on **all** employees, unless job-related.

Additional charge if cost (c) more than £75,000:

ORI × (c – £75,000)

Use market value if acquired > 6 years before provided

Official rate of interest at the start of the tax year

Job-related

- Necessary for proper performance
- For better performance and customary to provide
- Part of special security arrangements

Cars

Depends on car's CO_2 emissions and whether registered pre or post 6 April 2020

Max £5,000

Annual taxable benefit for private use of a car is:
(list price of car – capital contributions) × %.

- Refer to tax tables (max is 37%).
- Emissions 1 to 50g/km % dependent on electric range.
- % is 2% greater for cars registered before 6 April 2020.
- The % increases by 4% for diesel engined cars (max still 37%) unless they meet the RDE2 standard

The benefits are scaled down on a time basis, then the car and van (but **not** fuel) benefits are reduced by any contribution by the employee for private use. — payments to 'make good' by 6 July following the tax year

Vans

Unrestricted private use:

- 0g/km: £2,792
- >0g/km: £3,490

Fuel benefit:

- >0g/km: £666

Fuel – cars

- Fuel for private use is charged as percentage of base figure (£24,500 for 2020/21)
- Same percentage as car benefit
- No reduction for partial reimbursement by the employee

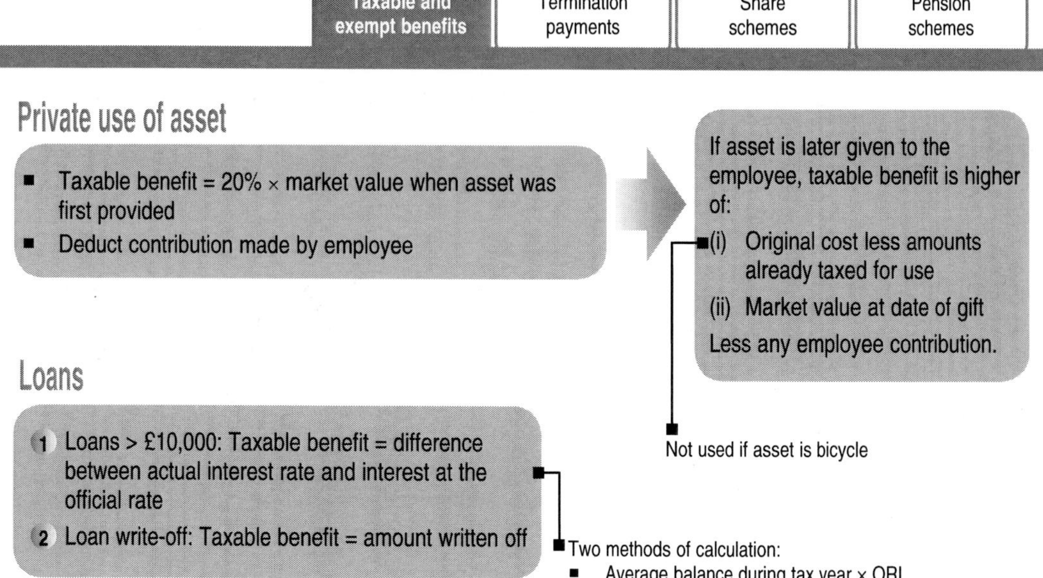

Private use of asset

- Taxable benefit = 20% × market value when asset was first provided
- Deduct contribution made by employee

If asset is later given to the employee, taxable benefit is higher of:

(i) Original cost less amounts already taxed for use

(ii) Market value at date of gift

Less any employee contribution.

Not used if asset is bicycle

Loans

1. Loans > £10,000: Taxable benefit = difference between actual interest rate and interest at the official rate
2. Loan write-off: Taxable benefit = amount written off

Two methods of calculation:

- Average balance during tax year × ORI
- Strict method: Actual balance × ORI

Exempt benefits

- Loans of up to £10,000
- Meals in staff canteen
- Workplace nurseries
- Job-related accommodation
- Medical insurance for overseas duties
- Mobile phone – restricted to one phone per employee
- Pension contributions to employer's registered scheme
- Relocation expenses of up to £8,000
- Additional household costs for homeworkers

Up to £6 per week may be claimed without supporting evidence

Expenses

- Include as general earnings
- Deduct if wholly, exclusively and necessarily incurred for performance of duties
- No need to report expense if would be fully allowable as deduction

Salary sacrifice

Taxable value of benefits where salary is sacrificed is higher of:

- Taxable value (using the benefits code); and
- Value of cash sacrificed.

Certain benefits excluded from this (eg, person savings and childcare)

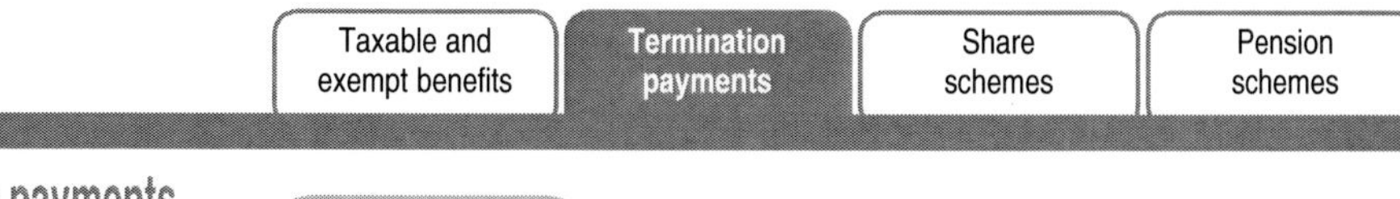

Termination payments

Termination payments can be a tax efficient method of rewarding employees on the termination of employment.

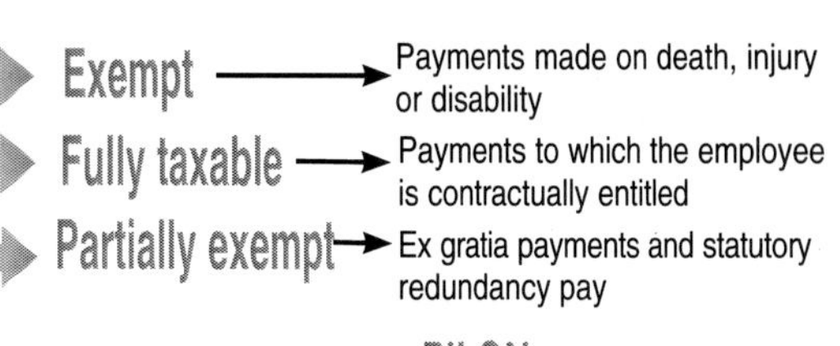

Partially exempt

Payments are fully taxable subject to an exemption for the first £30,000

↓

Taxed in year of receipt (not year when employment terminated)

↓

Non-cash benefits are valued using the normal benefit rules; some benefits are excluded eg, continued use of mobile phone

↓

From April 2020 Class 1A NIC payable on payments in excess of £30,000

PILON

- **Post-employment notice pay (PENP)**
  Occurs when employment is terminated during notice period.
  PENP is the basic salary that would have been earned if worked to the end of the notice period.
  PENP is taxable and NICable.
- **Balance of the PILON**
  This is (PILON - PENP)
  It is part of the termination payment subject to £30,000 exemption

Share option schemes – employees' tax liabilities

Corporation tax deduction usually available for employer

	Grant	Exercise	Disposal
Tax-advantaged scheme	Not taxable	Not normally taxable	Subject to CGT as normal
Other schemes	No tax for options granted after 1.09.03	Taxed as employment income: £ MV on exercise X Cost (X) Taxable X	Capital gain on increase in value of shares since exercise date: £ Proceeds X Cost (X) Amount charged to income tax on exercise (X) (Cost + amount charged: Equal to MV @ exercise) Gain X

Tax-advantaged schemes summary

	CSOP	EMI	SAYE	SIP
Qualifying employees	▪ Key employees only ▪ Own ≤ 30%	▪ Key employees only ▪ Own ≤ 30% ▪ Work for substantial amount of time for company	▪ Open to all employees ▪ No maximum holding	▪ Open to all employees ▪ No maximum holding ▪ Can award free shares based on performance
Max value at grant per employee	▪ £30,000	▪ £250,000 ▪ Reduced if also holds shares under CSOP ▪ Max £3m in issue	▪ Save £10 – £500 per month ▪ Buy out of post-tax income	▪ Free = £3,600 pa ▪ Partnership = £1,800 pa (max 10% salary) ▪ Matching = 2:1 ▪ Dividend = from SIP shares

	CSOP	EMI	SAYE	SIP
Conditions	▪ No discount at grant ▪ Exercisable between 3 and 10 years	▪ May issue at a discount ▪ Exercisable ≤ 10 years ▪ Trading company ▪ Gross assets ≤ £30m ▪ Quoted or unquoted ▪ < 250 employees	Maximum 20% discount	▪ Hold for at least 3 years ▪ Except partnership shares
Tax treatment at grant	No IT/NIC	No IT/NIC	No IT/NIC	▪ Free = No IT/NIC ▪ Partnership = Buy out of pre-tax income ▪ Matching = No IT/NIC ▪ Dividend = No IT on dividends used to buy more dividend shares

	CSOP	EMI	SAYE	SIP
Tax treatment at exercise	No IT/NIC	Taxable employment income if issued at discount: £ MV @ grant X Exercise price (X) Taxable X Use MV @ exercise (not grant) if lower result	No IT/NIC	N/A
Tax treatment at disposal	Normal CGT: £ Proceeds X Exercise price (X) Taxable X	Normal CGT: £ Proceeds X Exercise price (X) Taxable at exercise (X) Taxable X ■	Normal CGT: £ Proceeds X Exercise price (X) Taxable X	■ Still employee: No CGT ■ Not employee: Normal CGT £ Proceeds X MV when left plan (X) Taxable X

■ BADR available 2 years after grant of EMI option, even if own < 5%

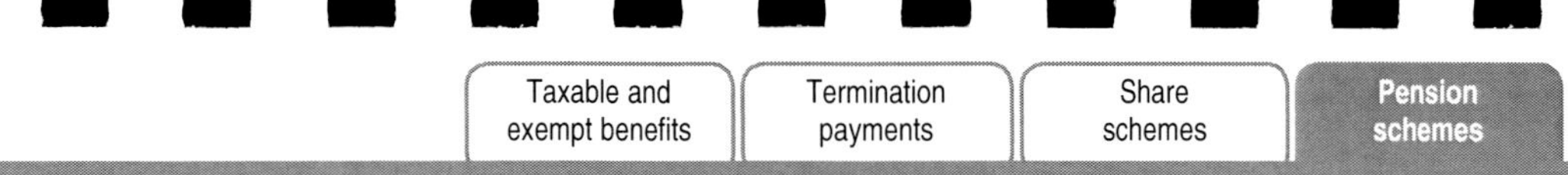

Pension schemes

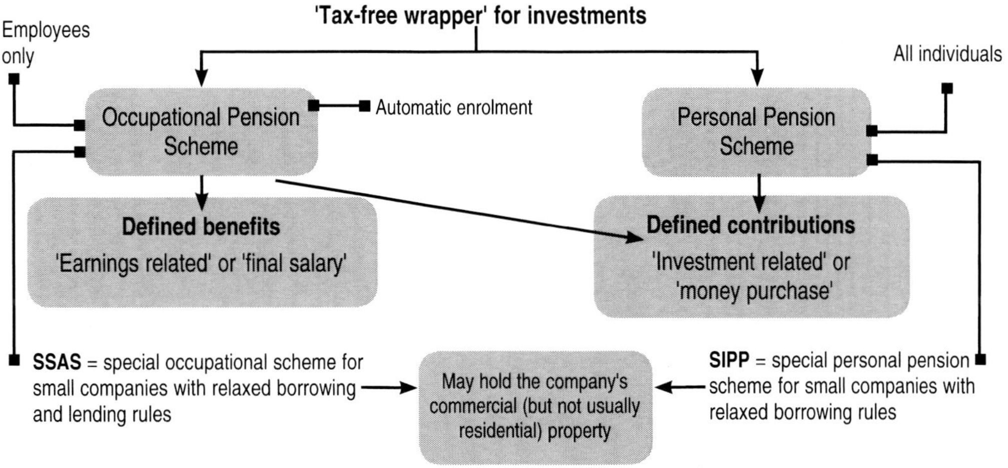

'Tax-free wrapper' for investments

Employees only

All individuals

Occupational Pension Scheme

Automatic enrolment

Personal Pension Scheme

Defined benefits

'Earnings related' or 'final salary'

Defined contributions

'Investment related' or 'money purchase'

SSAS = special occupational scheme for small companies with relaxed borrowing and lending rules

May hold the company's commercial (but not usually residential) property

SIPP = special personal pension scheme for small companies with relaxed borrowing rules

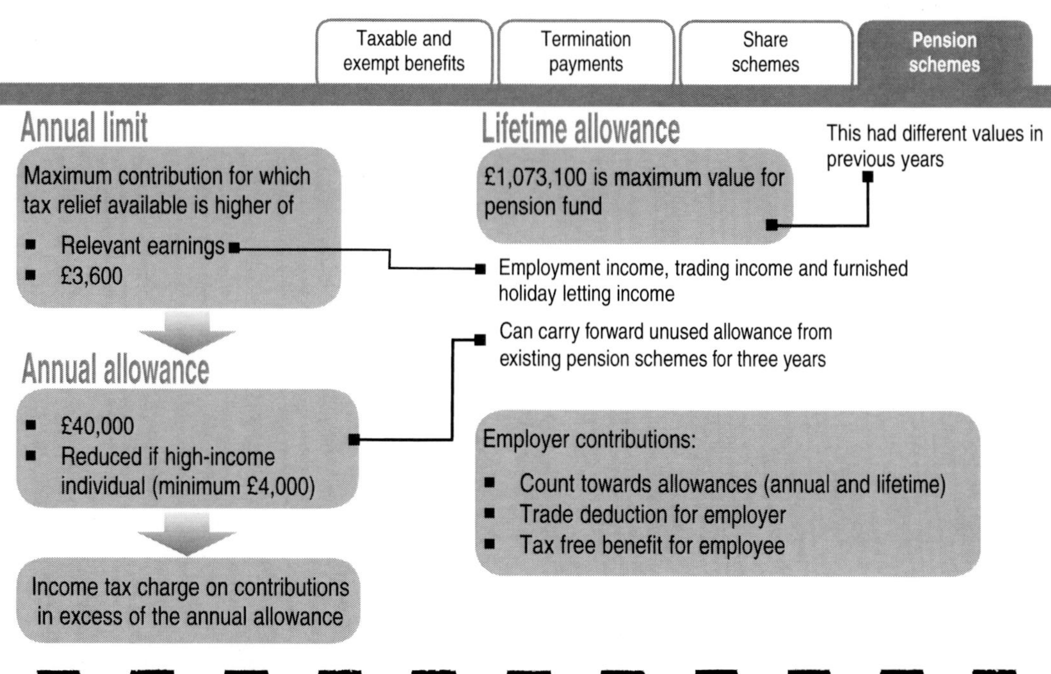
Taxable and exempt benefits
Termination payments
Share schemes
Pension schemes
Annual limit
Maximum contribution for which tax relief available is higher of
■ Relevant earnings
■ £3,600
Employment income, trading income and furnished holiday letting income
Annual allowance
■ £40,000
■ Reduced if high-income individual (minimum £4,000)
Can carry forward unused allowance from existing pension schemes for three years
Income tax charge on contributions in excess of the annual allowance
Lifetime allowance
£1,073,100 is maximum value for pension fund
This had different values in previous years
Employer contributions:
■ Count towards allowances (annual and lifetime)
■ Trade deduction for employer
■ Tax free benefit for employee

Tax relief

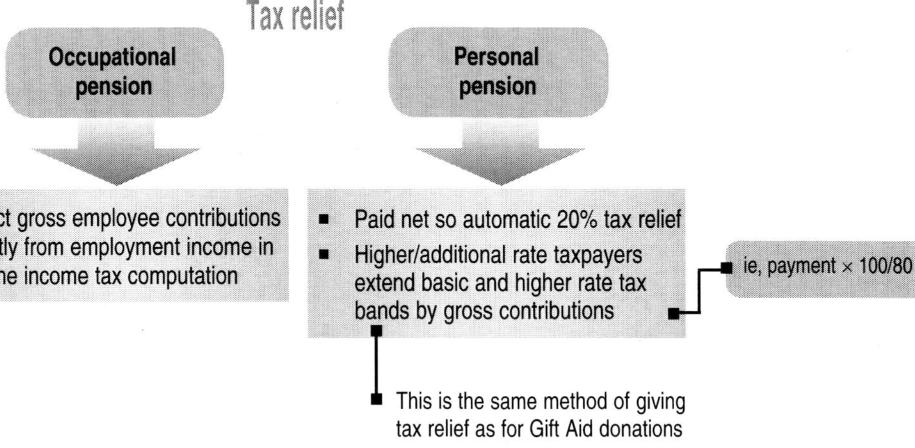

Occupational pension
Deduct gross employee contributions directly from employment income in the income tax computation
Personal pension
■ Paid net so automatic 20% tax relief
■ Higher/additional rate taxpayers extend basic and higher rate tax bands by gross contributions
ie, payment × 100/80
This is the same method of giving tax relief as for Gift Aid donations

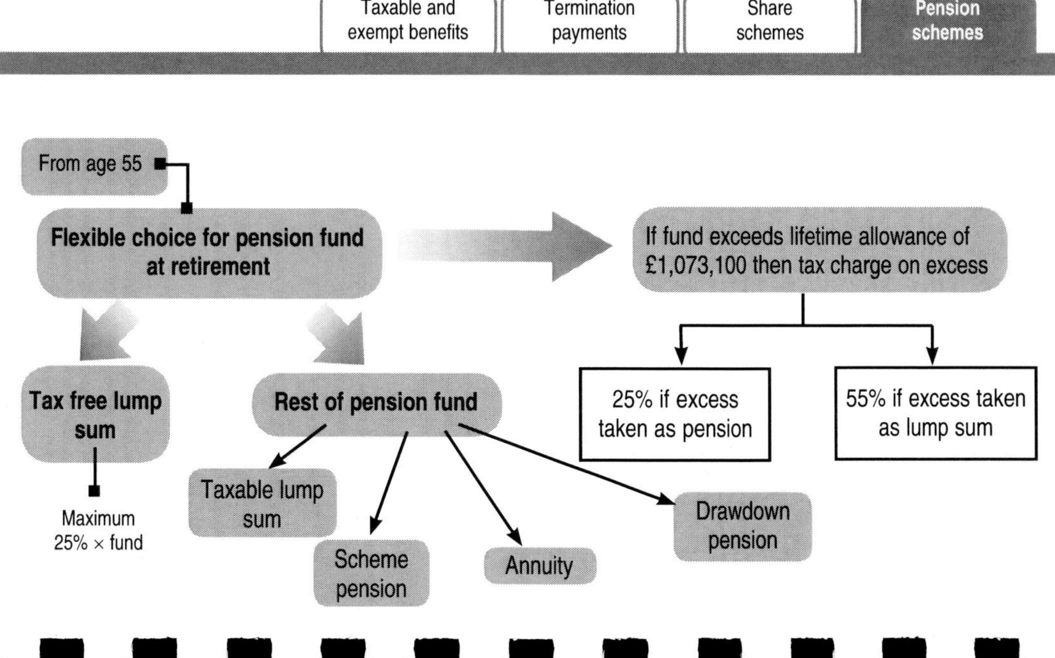
From age 55
Flexible choice for pension fund at retirement
If fund exceeds lifetime allowance of £1,073,100 then tax charge on excess
25% if excess taken as pension
55% if excess taken as lump sum
Tax free lump sum
Maximum 25% × fund
Rest of pension fund
Taxable lump sum
Scheme pension
Annuity
Drawdown pension

4: Unincorporated businesses

Topic List

Revision from Tax Compliance – calculation of trading profit/loss

Revision from Tax Compliance – relief for trading losses

Choice of loss relief

This chapter revises the rules you learned for your Tax Compliance exam. You need to be able to calculate the trading proft or loss, and identify the trading loss relief options for new businesses, businesses that have been trading a while, and those ceasing to trade or being incorporated.

Calculating the individual's taxable income after losses are relieved is also key, along with giving recommendations.

Adjustment of profits

To arrive at taxable trading profits, the net accounts profit must be adjusted.

- Certain items of expenditure are not deductible (ie, not allowable) for trading income purposes and must be added back to the net accounts profit when computing trading profits.
- Conversely other items are deductible (ie, **allowable**).

Allowable expenditure

Expenditure incurred **wholly** and **exclusively** for trade purposes

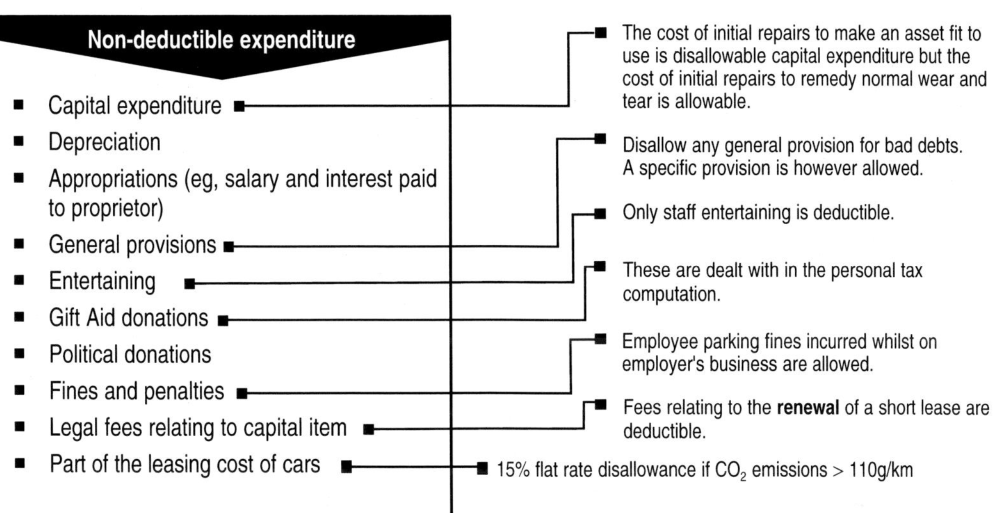

Non-deductible expenditure
Capital expenditure
Depreciation
Appropriations (eg, salary and interest paid to proprietor)
General provisions
Entertaining
Gift Aid donations
Political donations
Fines and penalties
Legal fees relating to capital item
Part of the leasing cost of cars
The cost of initial repairs to make an asset fit to use is disallowable capital expenditure but the cost of initial repairs to remedy normal wear and tear is allowable.
Disallow any general provision for bad debts. A specific provision is however allowed.
Only staff entertaining is deductible.
These are dealt with in the personal tax computation.
Employee parking fines incurred whilst on employer's business are allowed.
Fees relating to the **renewal** of a short lease are deductible.
15% flat rate disallowance if CO_2 emissions > 110g/km

Other adjustments

- Trading profits not shown in the accounts must be **added** — Eg, business owner takes goods for own use without reimbursing full market value, or receives payment in non-money form without including money's worth in accounts
- Non-trading income in the accounts must be **removed** — Eg, rental income, profits on the disposal of fixed assets and investment income
- Expenditure not shown in the accounts must be **deducted** — Eg, business expenditure paid personally by the owner

Pre-trading expenditure

Deductible on first day of trading providing:

- Incurred in the seven years prior to commencement of trade
- Would have been deductible trading expenditure if incurred after trade commenced

Fixed rate expenses

Can also choose to be taxed on the cash basis

Certain small businesses can, instead of actual expenses, deduct fixed rate amounts for:

- Motor vehicles
- Use of home for business purposes
- Business premises partly used as home

Current year basis (CYB)

The basis period for a tax year is normally the period of account ending in the year.

There are special rules which apply in the opening and closing years of a business

Opening years

Tax year	Basis period
1	**'Actual basis':** Date of commencement to following 5 April
2	Depends on length of accounting period ending in year 2: (a) 12 months: tax that 12 months (b) < 12 months: tax the 1st 12 months of trade (c) >12 months: tax the 12 months up to the accounting date (d) No accounting date ends in year: 6 April – 5 April ('actual' basis)
3	12 months to accounting date ending in year

Any profits taxed twice as a result of these rules = **'overlap profits'**

Relieved when:

- Business ends
- Change of accounting date

Closing year

Tax year that trade ends

- Basis period for the final year starts at the end of the basis period for the previous year and ends at cessation.
- Any overlap profits not already relieved are deducted from the final year's profits.

- If business ends in 1st tax year, tax all the profits
- If business ends in 2nd tax year, tax from 6 April until business ends

Capital allowances plant & machinery

Main pool

The main pool contains:

- All machinery, fixtures, fittings, equipment
- Vans, forklift trucks, lorries, motorcycles
- Cars with CO_2 emissions ≤ 110g/km

Writing down allowances (WDAs)

- 18% per annum on a reducing balance basis
- 18% × months/12 in a period that is not 12 months long
- Can claim less CAs than maximum possible

Balance = **tax written down value (TWDV)**

First year allowances (FYAs)

- Replace WDAs in period of expenditure
- **Not pro-rated in short/long accounting periods**
- Not usually available on cars

100% FYA available for:

- **New** low emission cars — CO_2 emissions ≤50g/km
- **New** zero emission goods vehicles
- Qualifying R+D capital expenditure
- Expenditure by **companies** in a designated enterprise zone
- Electric vehicle charging point

Annual Investment Allowance (AIA)

- For all businesses for expenditure up to £200k pa from 1 January 2021 (£1 million pa from 1 January 2019 to 31 December 2020).
- For AP straddling 1 January 2021 the AIA is calculated pro rata, but the max expenditure eligible after 1 January 2021 is £200,000 pro-rated for months post 1 January 2021
- Scaled up/down for long/short accounting periods of account
- Allocate AIA to assets eligible for **lowest** rate of WDA
- Balance of expenditure after AIA receives WDA

Special rate pool

Expenditure on:

- Long life assets (LLAs)
  - Expected economic working life 25+ years
  - Expenditure >£100,000 in period (pro rate for periods <12m)
- Integral features
  - Electrical systems
  - Cold water systems
  - Ventilation systems
  - Lifts
  - Escalators
  - Solar shading
- Thermal insulation and solar panels
- Cars with CO_2 emissions >110g/km

- WDA = 6% per annum on reducing balance basis
- Given after AIA if available
- Pro rate in a period that is not 12 months long

WDA for small pools

- If balance on main/special rate pool < small pool limit at end of chargeable period, can claim WDA up to small pool limit
- Small pool limit = £1,000 for 12 month chargeable period
- Pro rate for short/long periods

Private use assets

Assets used privately by the owner **not** an employee

- Keep each asset used privately by the business owner in a separate 'pool'
- AIA, FYA and WDA are calculated in full and deducted to calculate TWDV
- **But** can only claim the **business** proportion of allowances

Short life assets (SLA)

Not cars/assets with private use

- An **election** can be made to **depool main pool assets**
- Depooled assets must be disposed of within **eight years** of end of the period of acquisition
- From a planning point of view depooling is useful if balancing allowances are expected

Otherwise TWDV must be transferred to main pool

Pre-trading expenditure

- Eligible for capital allowances
- Treated as incurred on first day of trading

Cars – summary

- Cars with CO_2 emissions >110g/km
  - Special rate pool
  - WDA 6% per annum
- Cars with CO_2 emissions $\leq$110g/km
  - Main pool
  - WDA 18% per annum
- FYA for low emission car
- No AIA for cars

If private use asset, use CO_2 emissions to determine rate of WDA then apply private use asset rules

Balancing adjustments arise

On cessation to deal with balances remaining after deduction of disposal proceeds

- No WDAs/FYAs/AIAs on cessation

When a non-pooled asset is sold

When a column balance becomes negative

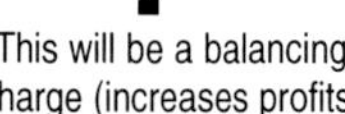

This will be a balancing charge (increases profits)

Successions

- If trade is transferred to a connected person assets transfer at TWDV, so no balancing adjustments.
- No WDAs, FYAs or AIAs in the period of disposal for the old owner; only WDAs for the new owner on the assets transferred

By joint election

Eg, – Incorporation
– Transfer to close relative

Balancing allowances

- Only arise in the main and special rate pools when trade ends

Structures and buildings allowance (SBA)

Eligible construction costs of new non-residential structures and buildings

- Construction of building (excl. land)
- Renovation or conversion of building
- Cost of new asset purchased from the developer (excl. land)

Allowances

SBA = Cost × 3% pa

- From first use
- Addition to building starts a new 33 1/3 year period for that new cost
- SBA apportioned for periods of less than or more than 12 months
- No balancing adjustment on sale (apportion allowances between vendor and purchaser)
- 2% pa SBA (pro-rated) before 1/6 April 2020.

Calculation of loss

Calculate trading income in the normal way. If it is negative then that amount is the loss for the year and taxable trading income is nil.

Alert! Losses in two overlapping basis periods are treated as losses of the earlier tax year only. Do **not** double count the losses.

Example

Sue starts trading on 1.10.19. Her losses are:

y/e 30.9.20 £(50,000)
y/e 30.9.21 £(20,000)

Losses for the tax years are:

2019/20

1.10.19 – 5.4.20 £(25,000)

2020/21

y/e 30.9.20 £(25,000) ie, £(50,000 – 25,000)

1st 12 months less the losses allocated to 2019/20

Carry forward (s.83)

A loss not otherwise relieved may be set against the first available profits of the same trade.

- Losses **must** be set against the first available profits: they cannot be saved up until it suits the trader to use them
- Losses may be carried forward for any number of years but if the trade changes, there is no further relief

Incorporation (s.86)

When a business is transferred to a company (ie, incorporated), pre-incorporation losses can be carried forward by the trader (not by the company) against the first available income he receives from the company.

- Consideration for the sale of the business must be wholly or mainly shares (80%)

Relief against general income (s.64)

Relief is against the general income of the tax year of the loss and/or the preceding tax year.

- Partial claims are not allowed: the whole loss must be set off, if there is income to absorb it in the chosen tax year.
- The trade must be carried on on a commercial basis with a view to the realisation of profits.

If claim against general income made can extend the claim to net chargeable gains of the same tax year, less brought forward capital losses.

Opening years (s.72)

A loss incurred:

- In the first **four** tax years of trade can be set against
- **Total income** of the **three** preceding tax years

Relief is given in the earlier year first (FIFO)

Closing years (s.89)

A loss incurred in:

- The last **12 months** of trade can be set against **trading profits** in
- The year of cessation and in the **three** preceding tax years

Relief is given in the later years first (LIFO)

Computation of terminal loss

		£
(a)	Actual trading loss for tax year of cessation (6 April to date of cessation)	X
(b)	Actual trading loss for period from 12 months before cessation to 5 April	X
Terminal loss		X

Include unrelieved overlap profits

If (a) or (b) yield a profit, assume the figure is nil.

Summary	s.83	s.64	s.72	s.89
Type of loss relief	CF	CY and/or PY (any order)	Loss in 1st 4 tax years	Terminal loss relief on cessation
Set against	Future trading profits from same trade	Total income	Total income	Trading profits from same trade
Time limits	CF until fully utilised or cease to trade	CY and/or PY	CB to previous 3 years on FIFO basis	CB to previous 3 years on LIFO basis
Conditions	■ Automatic ■ Cannot restrict to preserve PA	■ Optional ■ All or nothing ■ Claim in 1 or both years (any order)	■ Optional ■ All or nothing	■ Optional ■ All or nothing
Claim	Agree amount of loss within 4 years of end of tax year of loss	Within 12 months from 31 January following end of tax year of loss	Within 12 months from 31 January following end of tax year of loss	Within 4 years of end of last tax year in which business operated

Non-active traders

Loss relief restricted if:

- Individual does not devote significant amount of time to the trade during the loss-making period
  - At least 10 hours per week
- Maximum £25,000 loss if make s.64 or s.72 claim
  - s.64 and s.72 partnership and LLP losses also restricted in certain circumstances
- No restriction if CF

Tax avoidance schemes

If loss arises as result of tax avoidance arrangements, relief not available for:

- s.64
- s.72
- s.261B TCGA 1992 — Extension against gains

▸▸ see later

Restriction on income tax reliefs

Relief restriction for:

- Trading losses and property losses set against total income
- Interest on loan to invest in close company

▸▸ see later

Limited to higher of:

- £50,000
- 25% × adjusted total income

Considerations

- Income tax rate in relevant tax years
- Potential waste of loss where net income already covered by PA
- Potential waste of PA to achieve higher rate tax savings
- Projected level of future profits and tax rates

- Also type of income eg, are dividends covered by the dividend nil rate band?

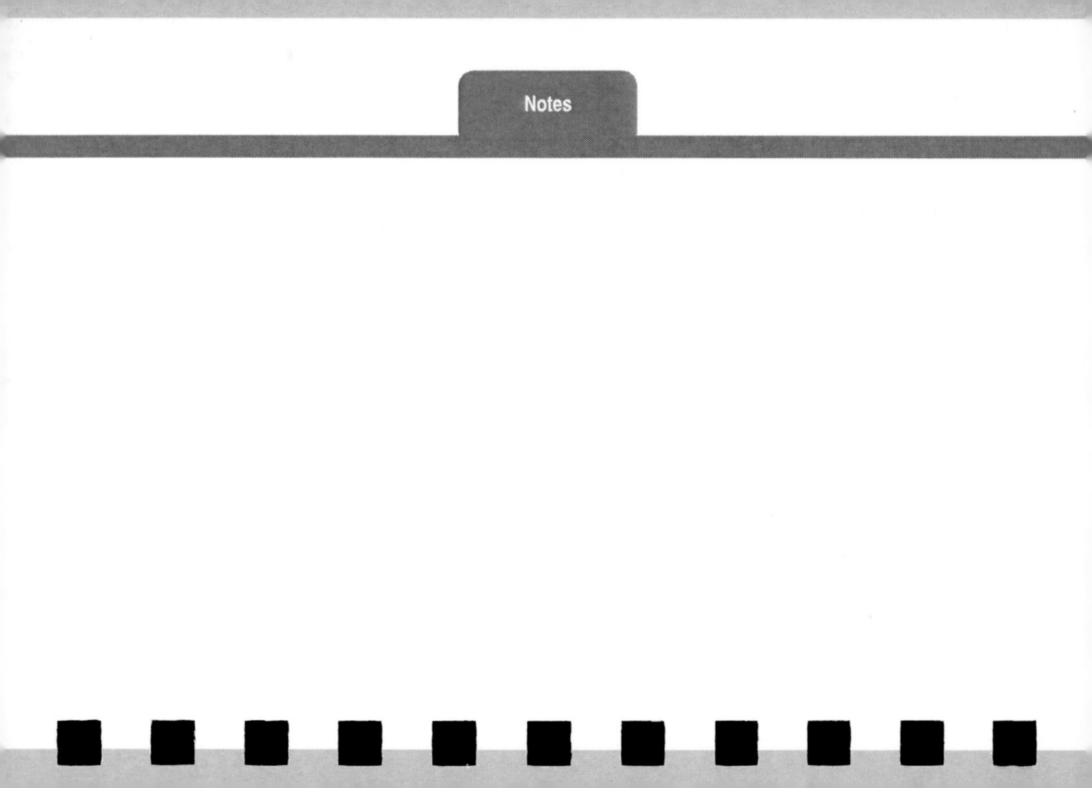
Notes

5: Capital gains tax

Topic List

You must be able to calculate gains as part of a personal tax question, often setting off gains and losses.

You should also be able to identify the option for relieving trading income losses against gains, and calculate the optimum form of loss relief.

You must also be able to advise an individual of capital gains tax planning opportunities within the family unit.

Chargeable persons, assets and disposals

Three elements are needed for a chargeable gain to arise.

1. A **chargeable person**: companies, individuals, partners and trustees are chargeable persons.
   - Charities and pension schemes are exempt from CGT
2. A **chargeable asset**: most assets wherever situated in the world are chargeable, but some assets are exempt.
   - Cars
   - Some chattels (eg, racehorses)
   - Gilts
   - ISA investments
3. A **chargeable disposal**: this includes sales and gifts. Transfer of assets on death is not chargeable.

Computation

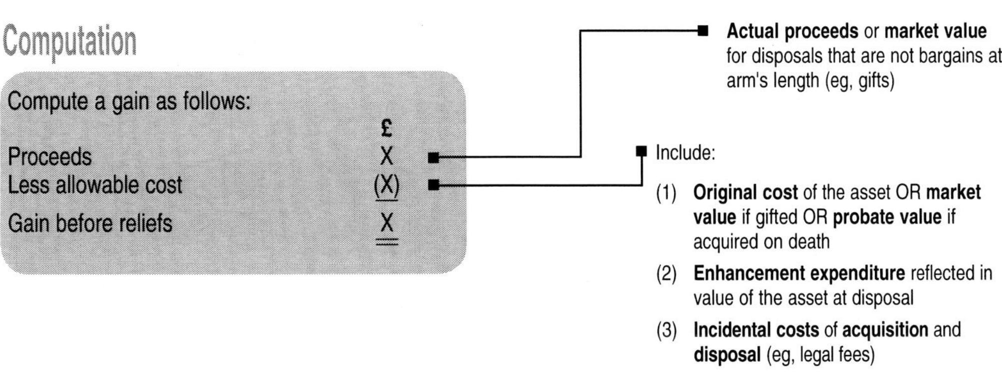

Part disposals

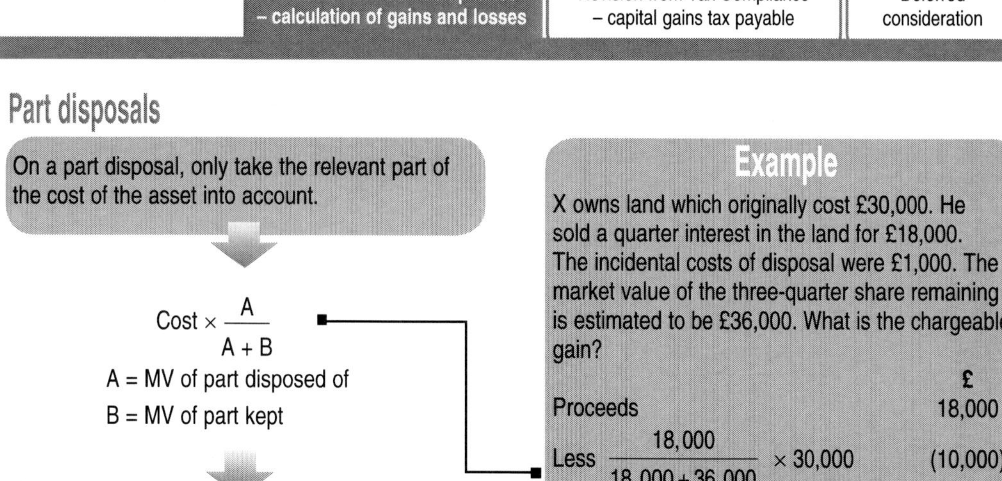

On a part disposal, only take the relevant part of the cost of the asset into account.

$$\text{Cost} \times \frac{A}{A + B}$$

A = MV of part disposed of

B = MV of part kept

Costs relating to the part disposal are deductible in full

Example

X owns land which originally cost £30,000. He sold a quarter interest in the land for £18,000. The incidental costs of disposal were £1,000. The market value of the three-quarter share remaining is estimated to be £36,000. What is the chargeable gain?

	£
Proceeds	18,000
Less $\frac{18,000}{18,000 + 36,000} \times 30,000$	(10,000)
Less incidental costs of disposal	(1,000)
	7,000

Spouses/civil partners

Transfers between them take place at no gain/no loss ie, proceeds = cost

Connected persons

- Transfers between connected persons (**relatives, business partners, settlor of a trust and its trustees**) take place at market value

Trustees are also connected to anyone connected with the settlor

Deduct allowable capital losses from chargeable gains in the tax year in which they arise.

Any loss that cannot be set off is carried forward to set against future chargeable gains.

Except losses on disposals to connected persons:

- Set only against gains on transfers to **same** person
- In same or future years

The net gains for the year are reduced by the annual exempt amount before then deducting any allowable losses brought forward.

Example

Zoë made chargeable gains of £14,000 in 2020/21. She had brought forward capital losses of £8,000.

The AEA of £12,300 reduces the gain to £1,700 allowing £1,700 of the brought forward capital loss to be set off in 2020/21. The remaining loss will be carried forward to 2021/22.

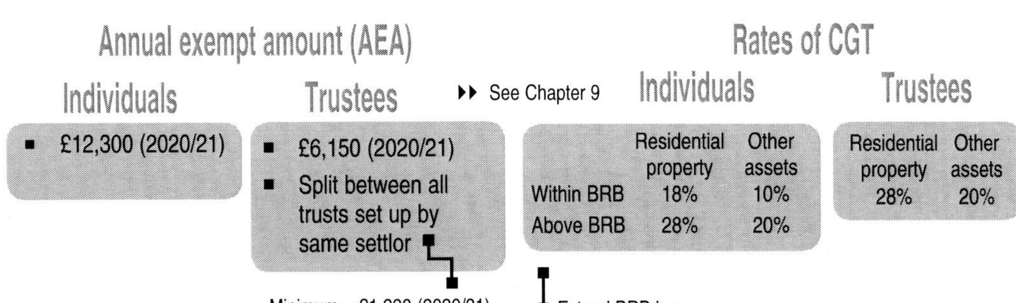

Business asset disposal relief

▸▸ See Chapter 6

- Reduces CGT payable on certain **qualifying business disposals**
- Gains qualifying for relief taxed at 10%
- Deduct losses and AEA so taxpayer pays least amount of tax
  - Residential property gains first
  - Then, other non-BADR gains
  - Then BADR gains
  - **But** BADR gains use up BRB in priority to non-BADR gains

Relief for trading losses against gains (s.261B)

Claim to set loss against the general income of:

- The tax year of the loss and/or
- The preceding tax year

- Can extend the claim for unrelieved part of the loss
- Set against chargeable gains of the same tax year as income tax claim

Available loss is **lower** of :

- 'Relevant' amount ie, unrelieved trading loss
- 'Maximum' amount ie:

	£
CY capital gain	X
Less CY capital losses	(X)
Less capital losses b/f	(X)
Maximum amount	X

Ignore AEA for these purposes (applies to: Less CY capital losses)

Deferred consideration

Payable in instalments

- Ignore fact that paid in instalments
- Tax full proceeds in tax year of disposal
- Can pay tax in instalments if instalment period >18m

Future payment conditional and known

- Ignore fact that consideration is conditional
- Include future proceeds in tax year of disposal
- If conditions not met in future, amend computation

Future payment conditional but unknown

- Proceeds include:
  - Actual proceeds received, and
  - Estimated net present value (NPV) of **right to receive the rest** ('Earn out')
- Receipt of future consideration is a disposal of that 'earn out' right
- Cost = original NPV
- If amount received < NPV, can carry back the loss arising (Individuals only)

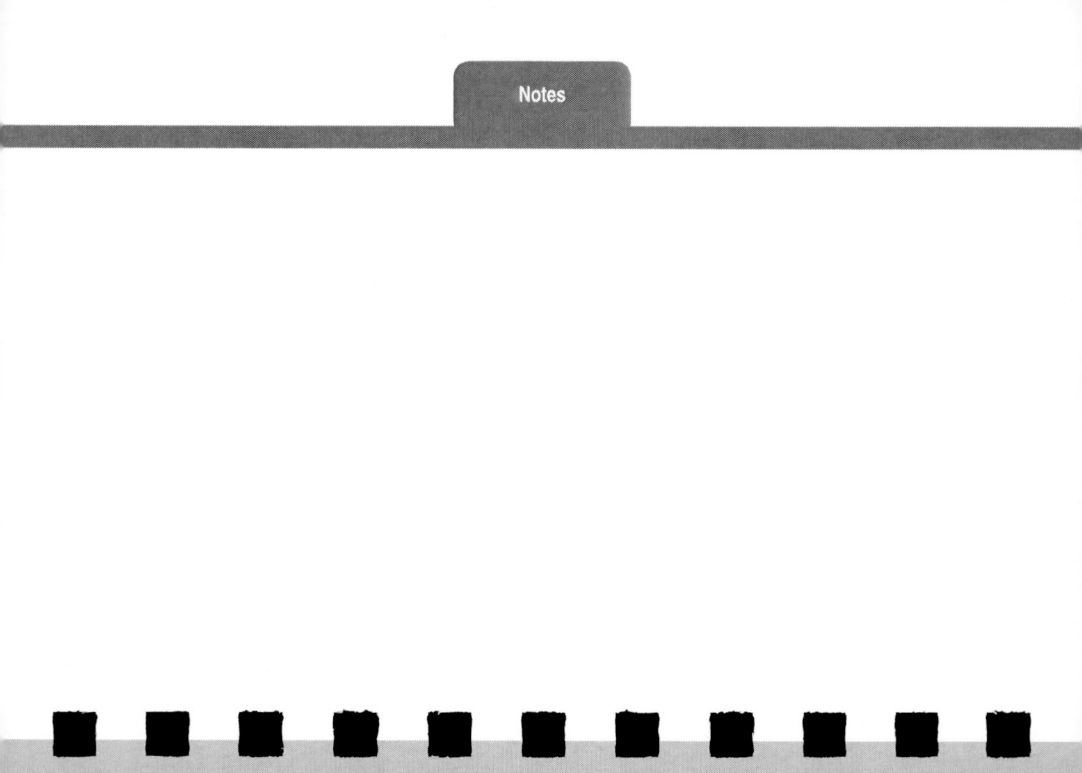
Notes

6: Capital gains tax – reliefs

Topic List

In advising businesses of their taxable gains you will be required to identify when business asset disposal relief, rollover relief, gift relief or incorporation relief apply.

You also need to be able to calculate the reliefs where specific restrictions apply, for example some non-business use for rollover relief.

Rollover relief

Taxpayers can claim to defer gains arising on the disposal of business assets that are being replaced if both the old and the new assets are on the list of eligible assets.

The new asset must be bought in the period starting **12 months before** and ending **36 months after** the disposal.

Exam focus

If a question mentions the sale of some business assets and the purchase of others, look out for rollover relief but do not just assume that it is available: the assets might be of the wrong type eg, moveable plant and machinery.

Eligible assets

- Land and buildings (including parts of buildings) occupied as well as used only for the purposes of the trade
- Fixed (that is, immoveable) plant and machinery
- Goodwill (individuals only)

A depreciating asset is one with an expected life of 60 years or less (eg, fixed plant and machinery).

Is the new asset a **depreciating** asset?
Is the new asset a **non-depreciating** asset?

For a **non-depreciating asset** the gain is **deducted from the base cost of the new asset**.

For a **depreciating asset** the **gain is deferred** until it crystallises at a later date.

If a part of the proceeds of the old asset are not reinvested, the gain is chargeable up to the amount not reinvested.

The gain crystallises on the earliest of:

1. The disposal of the replacement asset
2. Ten years after the acquisition of the replacement asset
3. The date the replacement asset ceases to be used in the trade

If a non-depreciating qualifying asset is bought before the gain crystallises, the deferred gain may be rolled into the base cost of that asset.

Non-business use

Relief is proportionately restricted when an asset has not been used for trade purposes throughout its life.

Alert! If any gain remains after rollover relief, business asset disposal relief may apply.

Gift relief

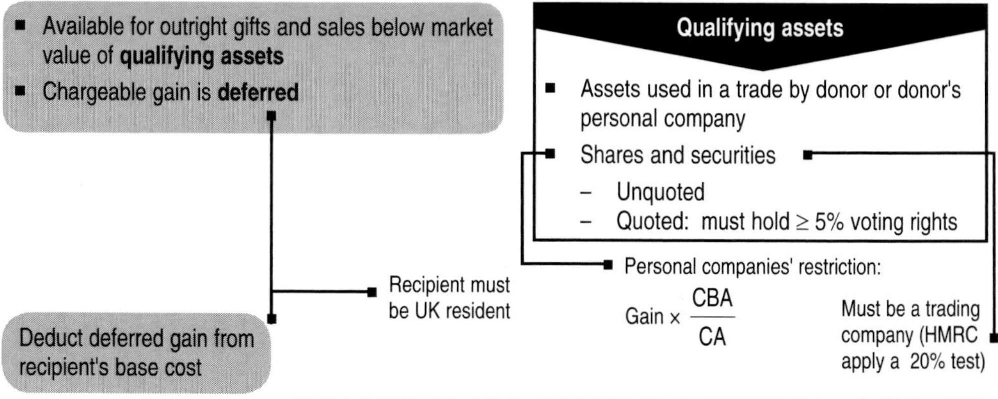

Alert! If any gain remains after gift relief, business asset disposal relief may apply.

Sales at below MV

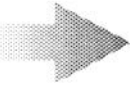

Receive actual proceeds but less than market value

Real profit is chargeable ie,:

	£
Actual proceeds received	X
Less actual cost	(X)
Gain chargeable now	X

Rest of gain is deferred by gift relief

Deduct this deferred gain from recipient's base cost

Business asset disposal relief

- Reduces CGT payable on certain **qualifying business disposals**
- Lifetime limit: **£1 million**
- Gains qualifying for relief taxed at 10%

Qualifying business disposal

(1) All/part of a trading business as a going concern (includes partnership interests)

(2) Assets which were used for the purposes of a business which has recently ceased

(3) Shares in the individual's personal trading company in which the individual is an employee

- Crystallise a gain to get BADR, where no longer a personal company due to a new share issue for cash (dilution of interest)
- Owns ≥ 5% of ordinary shares, voting rights, profits for distribution and assets on a winding up — Not required for EMI shares
- HMRC applies a 20% test to ensure 'trading'

Qualifying period of ownership

- (1) Owned business for two years before disposal
- (2) Owned business for two years before cessation and assets disposed of within three years of cessation
- (3) Qualifying conditions must have applied for two years before disposal — Runs from option **grant** date for EMI shares

Associated disposals

Disposal of individual business assets owned personally and used in a continuing trade only qualify for relief if:

1. Disposal of **partnership interest or qualifying shares;**
2. Individual makes disposal as part of **withdrawal from participation** in the business; and
3. Throughout a period of two years prior to the disposal the **assets are used for business purposes.**

eg, building owned personally but used by the partnership/company

if acquired on/after 13 June 2016 must have been owned for 3 years at disposal

at least 5% interest/ shareholding or entire shareholding if < 5%

Investors' relief

- Subscribe for new shares on/after 17 March 2016 — No minimum shareholding
- Unlisted trading company — Must not work for the company
- Held continually for 3 years before disposal

Incorporation relief

Relief applies when a sole trader or partnership sells/transfers their business to a company.

Applies automatically but can be disapplied by election.

Business must be transferred as a going concern.

All of the assets (or all except cash) must be transferred to the company.

The consideration must be at least partly shares.

The gain is deducted from the base cost of the shares instead of being immediately chargeable.

If only a proportion of the consideration is in the form of shares, relief is restricted to that proportion of the gain.

Alert! If any gain remains after incorporation relief, business asset disposal relief may apply (except for gain on goodwill transferred to a close company if owns $\geq$ 5% shareholding).

	Rollover relief	Gift relief
How does it work?	▪ Sell asset and acquire replacement ▪ Both used in trade ▪ Reinvest in 12m before or 36m after disposal	▪ Gift qualifying asset
What qualifies?	▪ Land and buildings ▪ Goodwill ▪ Fixed plant and fixed machinery	▪ Business asset ▪ Any unquoted trading co shares ▪ >5% quoted trading co shares
How much is the relief?	▪ Whole gain if all proceeds reinvested ▪ Otherwise proceeds not reinvested = chargeable	▪ Whole gain if no cash received ▪ Otherwise actual gain = chargeable ▪ CBA/CA restriction for shares
How is relief given?	▪ Non-depreciating: gain reduces new asset's base cost ▪ Depreciating: gain held over (max 10 years)	▪ Gain reduces donee's base cost

	Incorporation relief	Business asset disposal/Investors' relief
How does it work?	■ Transfer all business's assets except cash to limited company in return forshares	■ 10% CGT rate always applies
What qualifies?	■ Business assets if all transferred as a going concern	Business asset disposal relief: ■ Unincorporated business sale ■ Sale of shares in trading co if (a) 5% holding and (b) employee ■ Owned for two years Investors' relief: ■ Non-employee shareholders ■ Unlisted, trading company ■ Held > three years
How much is the relief?	■ Whole gain if no cash received ■ Otherwise gain relating to cash is immediately chargeable	■ Lifetime limit of £1m for Business asset disposal relief and £10m for Investors' relief eligible for 10% rate ■ Separate limit for each relief
How is relief given?	■ Gain reduces base cost of shares received	■ **Not** a deferral ■ Always tax gain at 10%

Interaction of reliefs

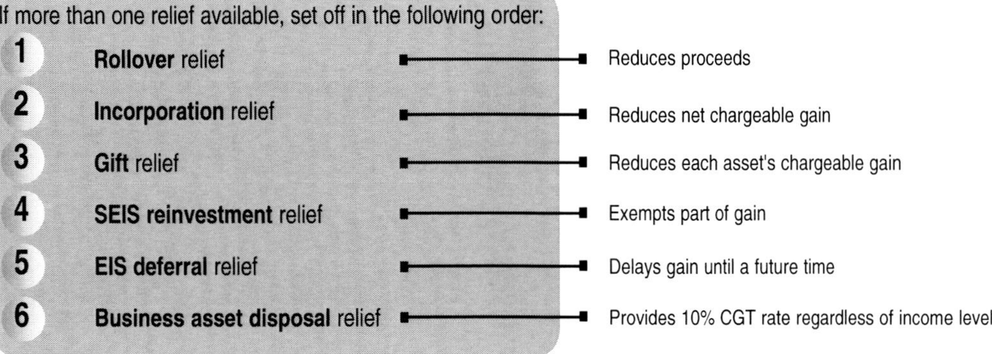

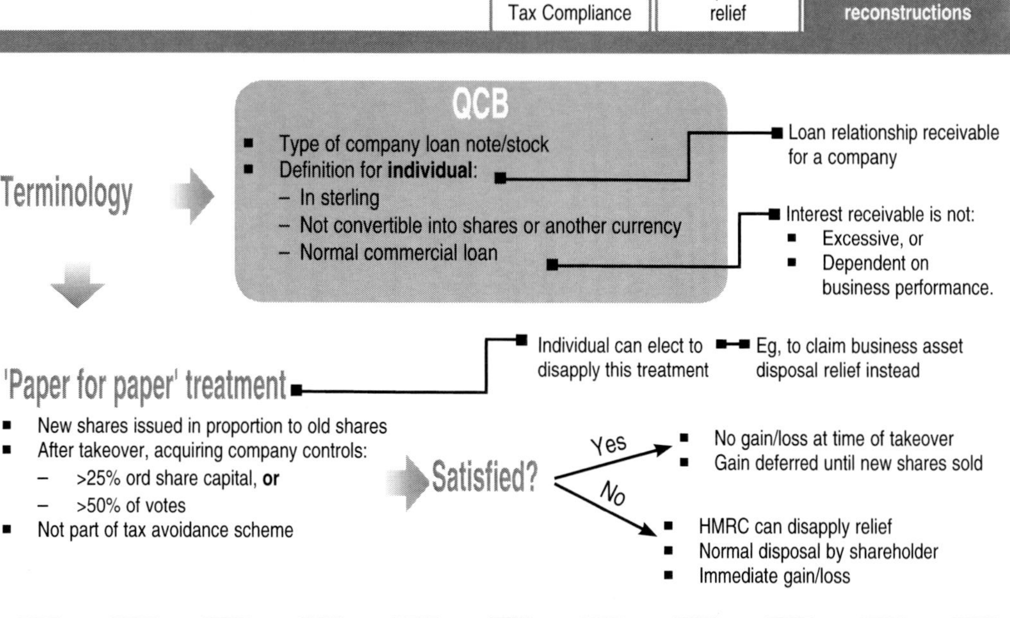
Terminology
QCB
■ Type of company loan note/stock
■ Definition for **individual**:
– In sterling
– Not convertible into shares or another currency
– Normal commercial loan
Loan relationship receivable for a company
Interest receivable is not:
■ Excessive, or
■ Dependent on business performance.
'Paper for paper' treatment
Individual can elect to disapply this treatment
Eg, to claim business asset disposal relief instead
■ New shares issued in proportion to old shares
■ After takeover, acquiring company controls:
– >25% ord share capital, **or**
– >50% of votes
■ Not part of tax avoidance scheme
Satisfied?
Yes
■ No gain/loss at time of takeover
■ Gain deferred until new shares sold
No
■ HMRC can disapply relief
■ Normal disposal by shareholder
■ Immediate gain/loss

Shares received in exchange for shares

- Same rules apply for non-QCB loan stock

- '**Paper for paper**'
- No gain/loss
- New holding deemed acquired on same date and at same cost as original holding

Shares and cash received

Proceeds = cash received

- Part disposal for cash element
- No gain for shares received
- Split base cost between cash (A) and shares (B) using: $\frac{A}{A+B}$

Qualifying corporate bond (QCB) received

- No gain for QCB element received
- **But** calculate gain and freeze it
- Charge frozen gain when QCBs disposed of

Actual gain/(loss) on disposal of QCB is exempt/(not allowable)

Notes

7: Inheritance tax

Topic List

- Revision from Tax Compliance
- Payment of IHT and interest
- Gifts with reservation of benefit
- Pre-owned assets
- Variations
- Interaction of IHT and CGT

This chapter covers how to advise on the use of business property relief and agricultural property relief in tax planning strategies for different individuals.

It also deals with HMRC's approach to gifts made with reservation of benefit and shows you how an individual's inheritance tax payable on death may be reduced by using a deed of variation.

You must also be able to identify when gift relief is available on lifetime transfers.

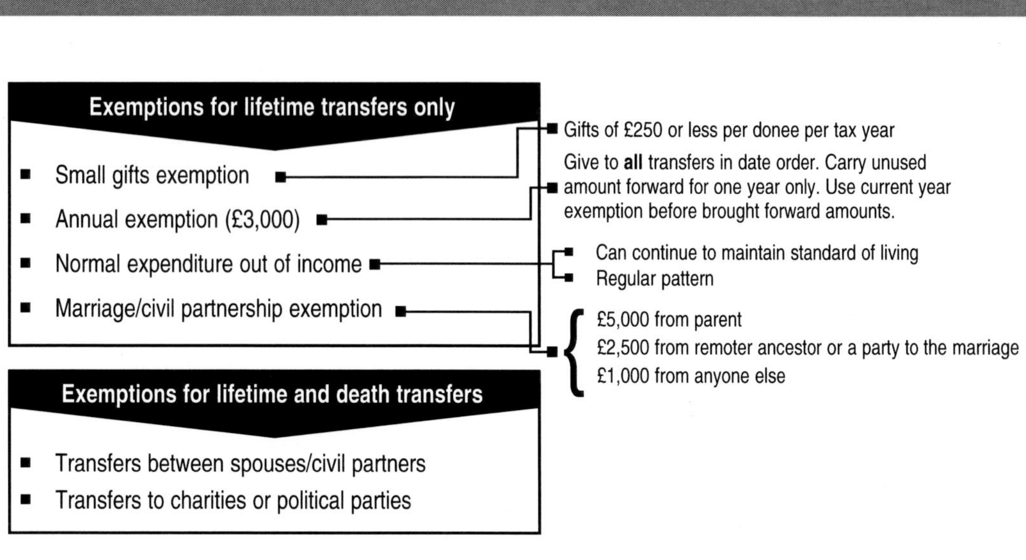
Exemptions for lifetime transfers only
Small gifts exemption
Annual exemption (£3,000)
Normal expenditure out of income
Marriage/civil partnership exemption
Gifts of £250 or less per donee per tax year
Give to **all** transfers in date order. Carry unused amount forward for one year only. Use current year exemption before brought forward amounts.
Can continue to maintain standard of living
Regular pattern
£5,000 from parent
£2,500 from remoter ancestor or a party to the marriage
£1,000 from anyone else
Exemptions for lifetime and death transfers
Transfers between spouses/civil partners
Transfers to charities or political parties

Assets are generally valued at their open market values.

Related property

Related property includes:

1. Property owned by the transferor's spouse
2. Property which the transferor or his spouse gave to a charity or political party in an exempt transfer, if the recipient has owned the property within the preceding five years

Related property is taken into account if doing so increases the value of assets

Diminution in value

Value before transfer	X
Value left with after transfer	(X)
Transfer of value	X

Special valuation rules

1. Value quoted shares and securities at the lower of:
   - The quarter up basis
   - The average of the highest and lowest marked bargains
2. Value unit trusts at the bid price (the lowest price).
3. Value of life insurance depends on whose death policy will pay out:
   - Deceased – maturity proceeds
   - Someone else – open market value
4. Land jointly owned
   - Related property – no deduction
   - Not related property – 5 – 15% deduction

HMRC's Shares and Assets Valuation department values unquoted shares

If written 'in trust' the policy is completely outside the deceased's estate

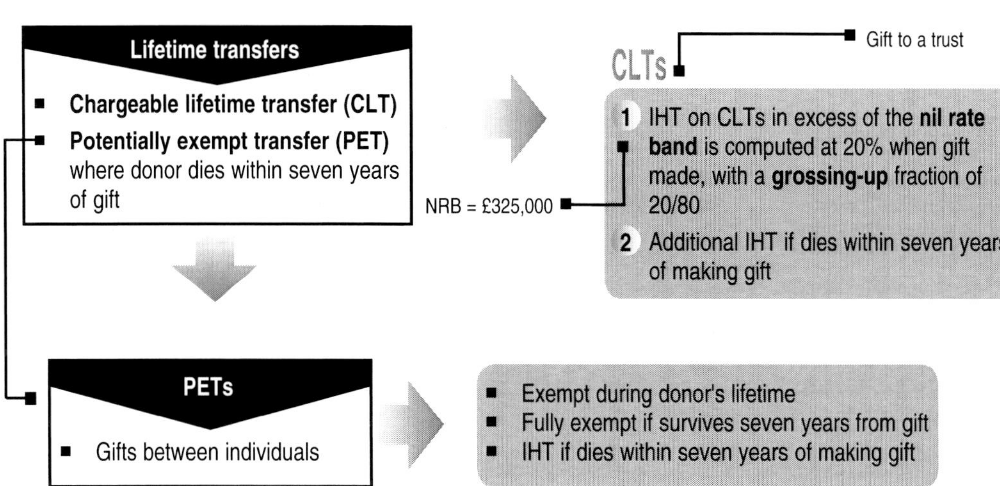
Lifetime transfers
Chargeable lifetime transfer (CLT)
Potentially exempt transfer (PET) where donor dies within seven years of gift
CLTs
Gift to a trust
1 IHT on CLTs in excess of the nil rate band is computed at 20% when gift made, with a grossing-up fraction of 20/80
NRB = £325,000
2 Additional IHT if dies within seven years of making gift
PETs
Gifts between individuals
Exempt during donor's lifetime
Fully exempt if survives seven years from gift
IHT if dies within seven years of making gift

Additional tax due on death

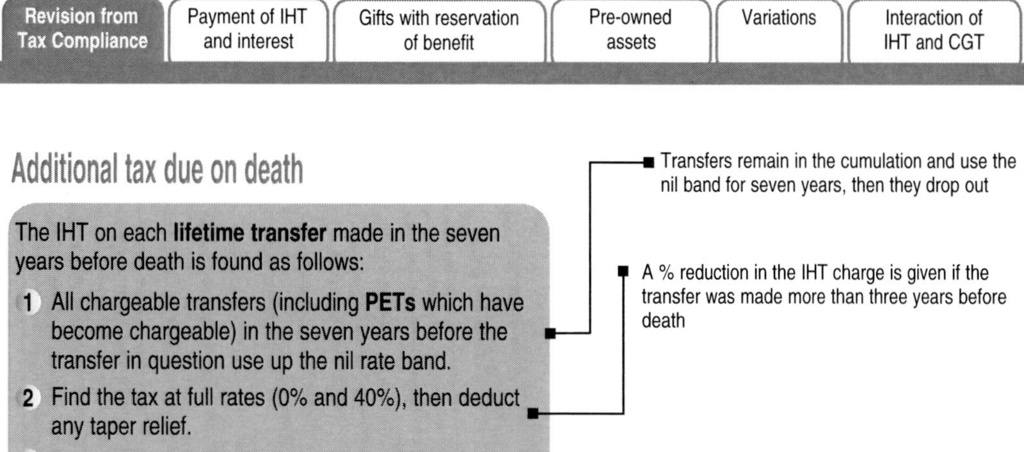

The IHT on each **lifetime transfer** made in the seven years before death is found as follows:

1. All chargeable transfers (including **PETs** which have become chargeable) in the seven years before the transfer in question use up the nil rate band.
2. Find the tax at full rates (0% and 40%), then deduct any taper relief.
3. Deduct any tax already paid on the transfer (CLTs only – no repayment available).

- Transfers remain in the cumulation and use the nil band for seven years, then they drop out
- A % reduction in the IHT charge is given if the transfer was made more than three years before death

Fall in value relief

If at date of donor's death a gifted asset has either:

1. Been sold for less than its MV when originally gifted

or

2. Is still held but is worth less than its MV when originally gifted

Deduct 'fall in value' from gross chargeable transfer (GCT)

Alert! Fall in value relief only affects the calculation of tax for the donee. It does **not** affect the donor's cumulative total.

Calculating death tax

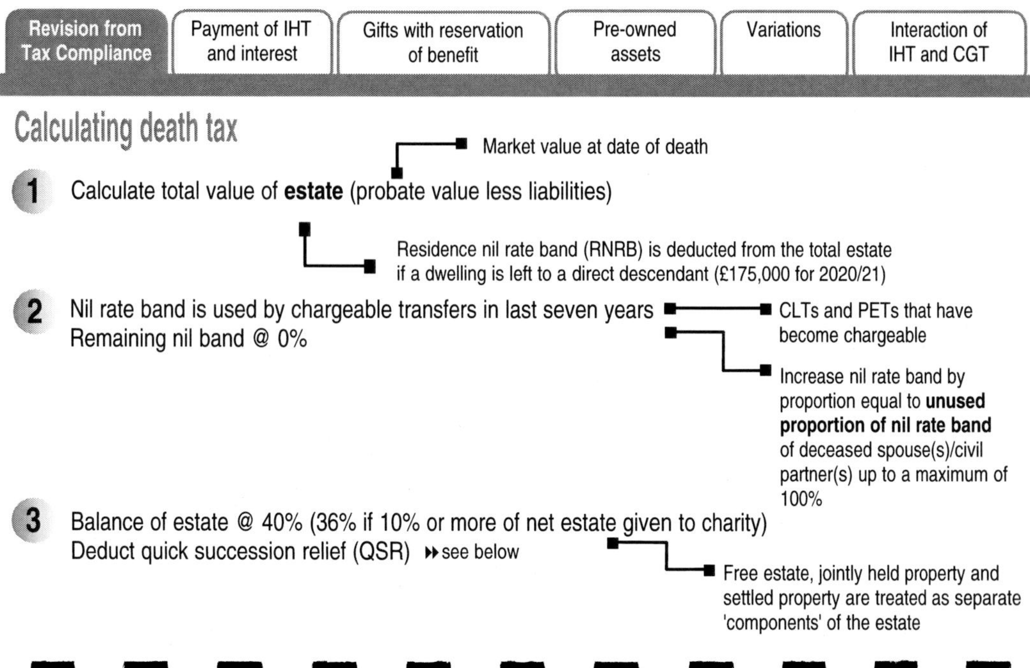

Quick succession relief (QSR)

QSR is given when someone dies within five years of receiving property in a chargeable transfer (the first transfer).

QSR is deducted from the IHT on the estate.

Period between transfers	% relief
1 yr or less	100
1 – 2 yrs	80
2 – 3 yrs	60
3 – 4 yrs	40
4 – 5 yrs	20
> 5 yrs	0

Computation

1. Take the tax paid on the first transfer, and multiply it by the net transfer/the gross transfer
2. Then multiply the result by a percentage, from 100% (for a gap of one year or less) to 20% (for a gap of more than four years)

Deemed domicile

Treat as UK domiciled for IHT:

- If resident in the UK for 15 out of previous 20 tax years
- A 'formerly domiciled resident'
  - Born in the UK
  - UK domicile of origin
  - UK resident in tax year of transfer
  - UK resident in one of two previous tax years

- UK domiciled – IHT on all assets wherever situated
- Non-UK domiciled – IHT only on UK assets

Double tax relief

DTR is available if property is situated overseas and suffers a foreign equivalent of IHT.

- DTR is the lower of the UK IHT on the asset (at the average rate) and the foreign tax.
- The DTR is deducted from the IHT.

Location of assets

- Immovable property – where situated
- Debts – where debtor resident
- Registered shares – where registered
- Bank account – where branch situated
- Goodwill – where business carried on

Transfers between spouses/civil partners

- Both UK domiciled: Completely exempt
- To non-UK domiciled spouse/CP: Exemption **limited** to value of nil rate band

Applies for IHT only (not IT or CGT)

UK domicile election

- Non-UK domiciled spouse/CP can make a UK domicile election
- Spouse exemption = unlimited
- But brings all overseas assets within scope of UK IHT

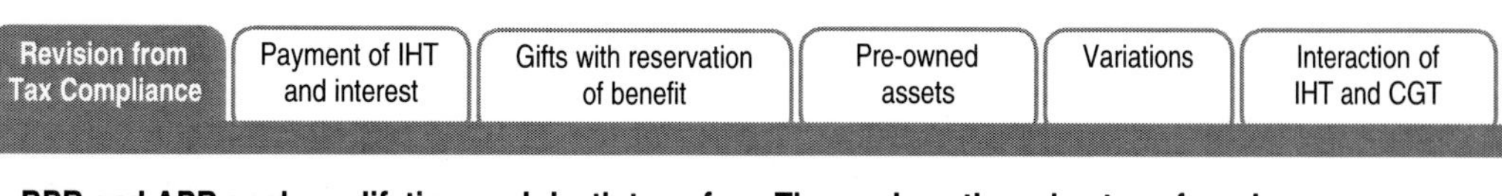

BPR and APR apply on lifetime and death transfers. They reduce the value transferred.

R elevant business property

BPR applies to transfers of:

1. Businesses
2. Unquoted securities where the transferor has control of the company
3. Unquoted shares (includes AIM listed shares)
4. Quoted shares or securities which gave the transferor control of the company
5. Land and buildings and plant and machinery used by the individual donor's partnership or company he controls.

- Businesses (1): Businesses of holding or dealing in financial investments or land are excluded
- Items 1–3: 100% relief → Watch for excepted assets
- Items 4–5: 50% relief

O wnership

The transferor must usually have owned the property for two years.

- Can combine certain shorter periods eg, if received on death of spouse

S ale contract

There must not be a binding contract for sale at date of transfer.

E xcepted assets

No relief for assets not used/needed in the business.

- Exclude investment assets/surplus cash

100% APR is available on most farm land and buildings in the UK or elsewhere in the EEA.

- Only the agricultural value qualifies. The balance of the value, and the value of plant and machinery, may get BPR.
- 50% relief only for:
  - Tenanted land;
  - Lease granted before 1 September 1995; and
  - Lease has > two years left to run.

APR conditions

The transferor must have usually:

1. Occupied the property for agricultural purposes for two years; or
2. Owned the property for seven years, during which time someone occupied it for agricultural purposes.

Farming companies

Shares and securities owned by an individual who controls a farming company qualify if:

1. The company would qualify for APR on a transfer of its land; and
2. The shares or securities have been owned for two years or seven years respectively.

Liabilities

Deduct liabilities relating to APR/BPR property before deducting APR/BPR

Withdrawal of BPR and APR

For **lifetime transfers**, BPR and APR do not apply when computing the tax on death if:

1. The donee has sold/gifted the property before the donor's death.
2. The donee still owns the property but is not using it for business/agricultural purposes.
3. The property is no longer relevant business/agricultural property.

Unless full proceeds of sale used to buy qualifying replacement property

Eg, unquoted shares have become quoted (and the donee does not control the company)

Instalment payments

- IHT on certain property can be paid in ten equal annual instalments on CLTs where tax is borne by the donee, or on the death estate.
- Additionally, IHT due on PETs as a result of the death of the donor can be paid in instalments.

Land and buildings
Most unquoted shares and securities
Business/interest in business

Interest-free instalments

Not investment/property trading companies

No interest, if paid on time, on:

1. Controlling holdings in quoted shares/holdings in unquoted shares
2. BPR qualifying sole trader businesses and partnership interests
3. Land eligible for APR/BPR – part not covered by relief

Interest-bearing instalments

Interest on outstanding balance on:

1. Non-BPR holdings in shares
2. Non-BPR qualifying sole trader businesses and partnership interests
3. Land not qualifying for APR/BPR

Gift with reservation

A **gift with reservation** is, broadly, a gift where the donor retains some interest in the gift.

1. The gift is treated as a PET or CLT when made.
2. The gift is also either included in the death estate or treated as a PET or CLT when the reservation ceases.

The higher of the two IHT charges in (1) and (2) above is made.

The three **exceptions** to the rule are:

- When the donor gives full consideration for the reserved benefit
- When the property is land and the reservation arises because of an unforeseen change in the circumstances of the donor, being an elderly or infirm relative of the donee
- Virtual exclusion

Eg, < three lifts per month in gifted car

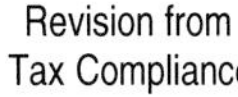

Pre-owned assets tax charge (POAT charge)

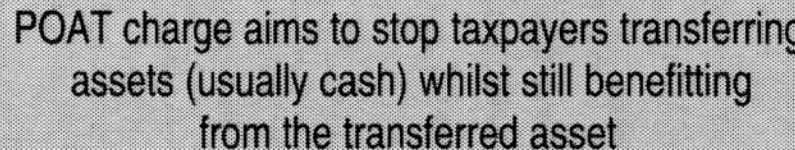

POAT charge aims to stop taxpayers transferring assets (usually cash) whilst still benefitting from the transferred asset

Eg, A parent gives cash to an adult child. The adult child uses the cash to purchase a house that the parent then lives in rent free.

POAT charge is an income tax charge
'Notional income' x transferor's marginal rate

- 'Notional income' is annual market rent where a house is purchased with the cash transferred
- No POAT charge if
  - notional income does not exceed £5,000
  - transfer is to a spouse
  - cash transfer was more than 7 years before the asset was first used
  - transferor elects to use GWROB

Variations

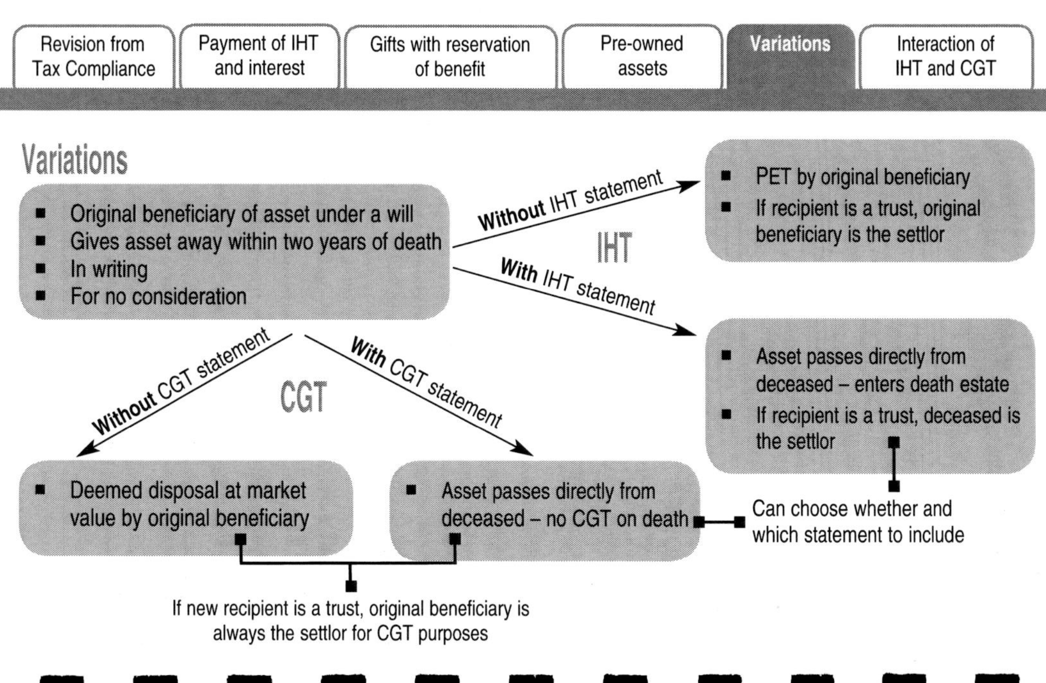
Original beneficiary of asset under a will
Gives asset away within two years of death
In writing
For no consideration
Without IHT statement
IHT
With IHT statement
PET by original beneficiary
If recipient is a trust, original beneficiary is the settlor
Asset passes directly from deceased – enters death estate
If recipient is a trust, deceased is the settlor
Without CGT statement
CGT
With CGT statement
Deemed disposal at market value by original beneficiary
Asset passes directly from deceased – no CGT on death
Can choose whether and which statement to include
If new recipient is a trust, original beneficiary is always the settlor for CGT purposes

	CGT	IHT
Payable	▪ Chargeable disposals by chargeable persons during lifetime ▪ Some assets = exempt ▪ Not payable on death (tax free uplift to MV) ▪ Planning: transfer appreciating chargeable assets on death	▪ Lifetime: CLTs ▪ On death: PETs and CLTs < 7 yrs of death; all assets owned at death ▪ No exempt assets ▪ Some gifts are exempt eg, to spouse/charity/political parties
Inter-spouse/CP transfers	▪ No gain/no loss	▪ Transfers exempt both in lifetime and on death ▪ Can transfer unused nil rate band
Related property	▪ No concept for CGT ▪ Value assets at their stand alone value (usually MV)	▪ Value assets based on ownership of donor plus holdings of related property ▪ Also consider loss to donor ie, reduction in value of donor's estate as result of transfer

	CGT	IHT
Transfers that are PETs	■ If a chargeable asset = liable to CGT **unless** qualifies for gift relief ■ s.165 TCGA 1992 gift relief applies to business assets (s.260 cannot apply as no immediate charge to IHT on a PET) ■ Business asset disposal relief may be available	■ No IHT during lifetime ■ IHT may become payable if donor dies < 7 years after making gift ■ Taper relief if donor surivives at least 3 years after making gift
Transfers that are CLTs	■ If a chargeable asset = liable to CGT ■ s.260 gift relief applies to **any** asset as also immediate charge to IHT (even if within NRB) ■ Business asset disposal relief may be available if gift relief not claimed	■ Lifetime IHT @ 20% if not covered by NRB ■ Further IHT may become payable if donor dies < 7 years after making gift ■ Taper relief is available if made at least 3 years before death
Gift with reservation of benefit	■ If a chargeable asset = liable to CGT ■ If house gifted and not occupied by donee, no private residence relief	■ PET/CLT and also included in donor's estate ■ Choose treatment resulting in higher tax liability (usually death estate)

8: Personal tax – international aspects

Topic List

Revision from Tax Compliance

Tax planning

You must be able to suggest potential tax planning strategies suitable for a particular individual.

This chapter helps you to advise an individual on whether he should make a claim to use the remittance basis.

It also considers the implications of a person's residence and domicile status for a potential or past transaction.

Domicile

- Country of permanent home
- Three main types of domicile:
  - Origin
  - Dependency
  - Choice

Can only change domicile by:

- Severing ties with the old country; and
- Establishing a permanent life in the new country.

Deemed domicile applies for IT and CGT (differs to IHT definition)

Deemed domicile

Deemed domiciled for IT/CGT if:

- UK resident at least 15 of previous 20 tax years, or
- Non-domicile but
  - born in UK and
  - UK domicile of origin and
  - UK resident in current year

UK resident but non-UK domiciled individuals can claim to be taxed on overseas income only when it is **remitted** to the UK.

ie, '**remittance basis**'

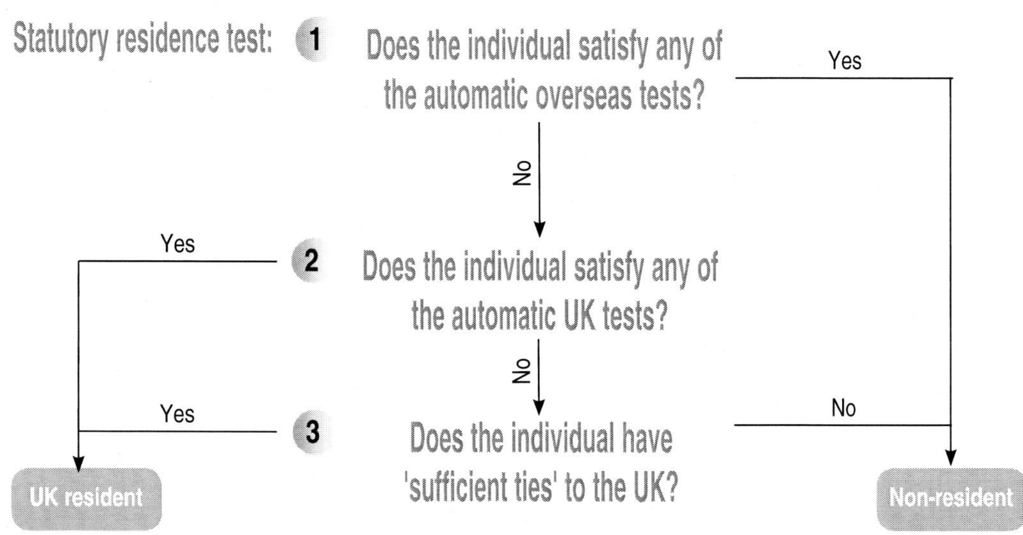

Statutory residence test:
1 Does the individual satisfy any of the automatic overseas tests?
Yes
No
2 Does the individual satisfy any of the automatic UK tests?
Yes
No
3 Does the individual have 'sufficient ties' to the UK?
Yes
No
UK resident
Non-resident

Automatic overseas tests

- Resident in one of last three years and spends < 16 days in UK
- Not resident in any of last three years and spends < 46 days in UK
- Works full-time overseas
  - 35 hours per week overseas
  - Breaks in overseas work ≤ 30 days
  - < 31 UK work days
  - < 91 days in UK

Automatic UK tests

- Spends at least 183 days in UK
- Period of ≥ 91 consecutive days during which:
  - Only home is in the UK and visits for ≥ 30 days in tax year; or
  - Has both UK and overseas home but visits to overseas home < 30 days in tax year
- Works full-time in UK

Over 365-day period (all/part in the tax year):

- 35 hours per week in the UK
- Breaks in UK work < 31 days
- > 75% UK work days
- Works in UK at least one day in the tax year for three hours

Within the 365 day period

Ties

May be able to split the tax year ▸▸ see later

- Family
- Accommodation
- Work
- 90 days
- More time in the UK than elsewhere?

Only consider final tie if was resident in at least one of the three previous tax years

Days in UK in tax year	Leavers	Arrivers
0 – 15	Not resident	Not resident
16 – 45	Resident if 4 ties	Not resident
46 – 90	Resident if 3 ties	Resident if 4 ties
91 – 120	Resident if 2 ties	Resident if 3 ties
121 – 182	Resident if 1 tie	Resident if 2 ties
183 or more	Resident	Resident

Splitting the tax year

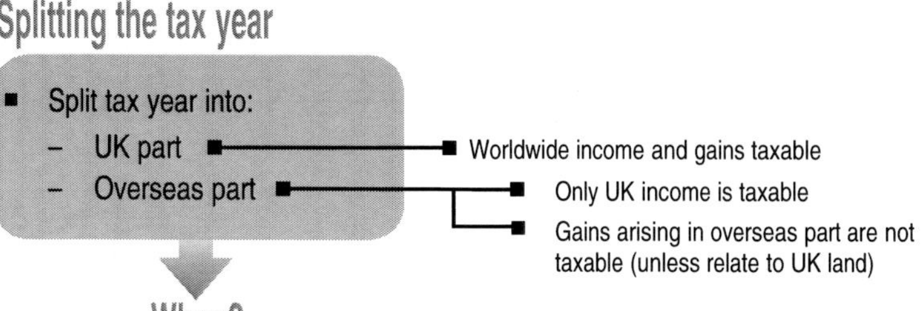

Leavers

- He (or spouse) starts full-time work overseas
  ▸▸ see later
- Ceases to have a UK home

Arrivers

- He (or spouse) starts full-time work in the UK
- He (or spouse) returns from full-time work overseas
- Acquires UK home or UK home becomes his only home

Remittance basis

Income taxed only when brought into the UK

If individual is:

- Non-UK domiciled; and
- Has foreign income.

Foreign income taxed on arising basis unless remittance basis claimed.

Remittance basis **automatically** applies if the individual has:

- Unremitted income/gains in tax year < £2,000; or
- No UK gains and UK investment income ≤ £100 which has been taxed in the UK **and** makes no remittances in the tax year **and** either aged < 18 or been resident in UK for not more than 6 years out of last 9.

Applies if deemed domicile, but otherwise cannot claim RB

If remittance basis is **claimed**:

- No personal allowance
- £30,000 RBC if UK resident for ≥ 7 years out of previous 9 tax years **and** aged >18 years

RBC increases to:

- £60,000 when resident for ≥ 12 out of previous 14 tax years

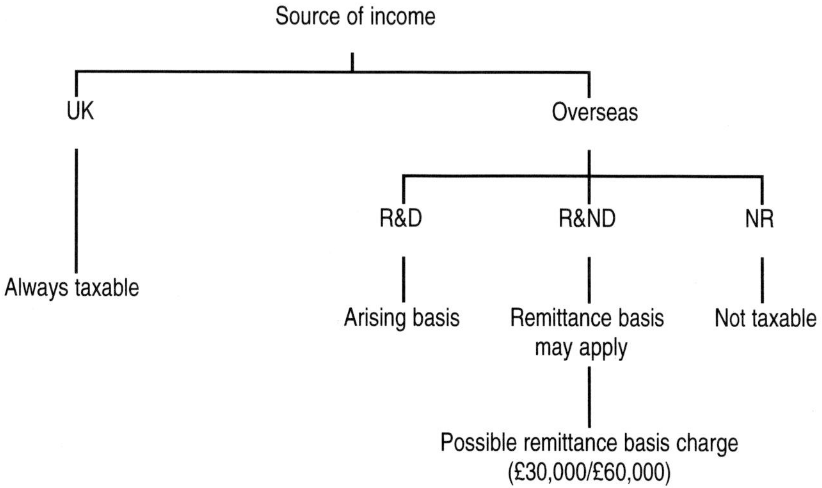

Source of income

- UK
  - Always taxable
- Overseas
  - R&D
    - Arising basis
  - R&ND
    - Remittance basis may apply
      - Possible remittance basis charge (£30,000/£60,000)
  - NR
    - Not taxable

Employment income

1 Resident and domiciled in UK

Taxable on **worldwide** earnings

2 Resident but not domiciled

- Taxable on **worldwide** earnings in UK
- **But** may claim **remittance** basis for overseas earnings if employer non-UK resident

3 Not resident in UK

- UK earnings taxed in UK
- Foreign earnings **not** taxable

Other income

- **Foreign dividends** – taxed in the same way as UK dividends
- **Overseas interest** – taxed in the same way as UK savings income
- **Overseas trade** – profits calculated as for UK trade
- **Overseas rental income** – taxed in same way as UK rental income

Taxed on **arising** basis unless the **remittance** basis applies ie, if the individual is not domiciled in the UK.

If remittance basis applies, all income, including dividends and interest, is taxed as **non-savings** income.

Double tax relief is given to prevent income being taxed in both the UK and overseas.

1 Agreements

Relief may be given under an agreement between the two countries.

If no agreement →

2 Credit relief

- Foreign income brought into the tax computation gross
- Treated as the **top slice** of individual's income
- Relief = lower of:
  - The foreign tax; and
  - The UK tax.
- Deduct from the UK tax

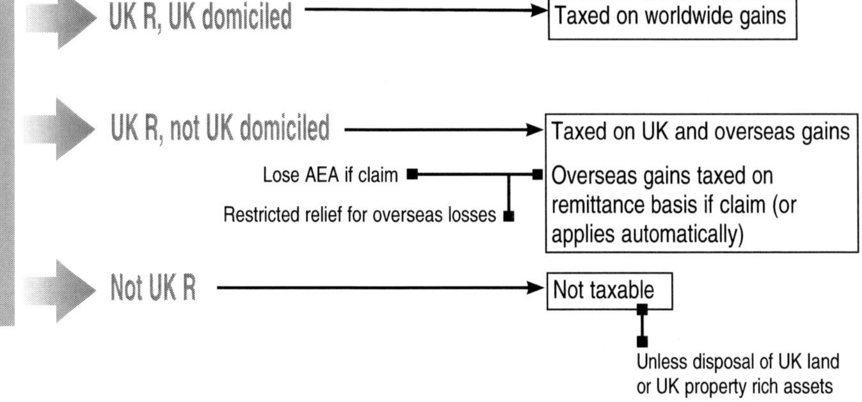
Overseas aspects of CGT
UK R, UK domiciled
Taxed on worldwide gains
UK R, not UK domiciled
Taxed on UK and overseas gains
Overseas gains taxed on remittance basis if claim (or applies automatically)
Lose AEA if claim
Restricted relief for overseas losses
Not UK R
Not taxable
Unless disposal of UK land or UK property rich assets

Double taxation relief (DTR)

Available if gain taxed both in UK and overseas

Calculated based on sterling figures

Relief for lower of UK and overseas tax

Deemed UK domicile - in gain calculation use MV at 5.4.17 (instead of cost) for assets held at 5.4.17

Residential property-CGT on post 5 April 2015 gain

Non-residential/property rich asset – CGT on post 5 April 2019 gain

Return/pay within 30 days

TP06-34220-062

Overseas employment

If conditions satisfied, can split the tax year into UK and overseas parts if leave during the year to work full time overseas

Tax free overseas employment expenses

- Overseas board and lodgings
- Any number of visits home
- Travel costs for up to 2 return visits of spouse and minor children if period of absence at least 60 continuous days

Planning considerations when employed abroad

- Timing – stay outside UK for required time period
- Separate income and capital funds if remittance basis applies
- Claim to receive bank interest gross NRs cannot contribute to ISAs

Must choose whether:

- To claim to use remittance basis and (maybe) pay RBC, lose PA and AEA
- Not claim and pay tax on all UK and overseas income as normal

CGT planning

- May be able to split the tax year for CGT purposes
- Watch for temporary non-residence rules if do not remain outside the UK for five years or more

▸▸see later

- Remittance basis (RB) for CGT available to non-UK domiciled individuals
- RB users must make irrevocable election in first year of using RB to be able to use **overseas losses**

Exemptions available if:

- Invest funds within 45 days of bringing them into UK
- Bring asset to UK for sale and send proceeds overseas within 45 days

Must offset losses in set order ie, against:

1. Remitted overseas gains
2. Unremitted overseas gains
3. UK gains

Temporary non-residence

Cash flow advantage?

- Individual becomes non-resident;
- Was UK resident for four out of seven tax years before leaving the UK; and
- Remains non-resident for five or fewer complete years.

Income

Certain foreign income received or remitted to the UK while temporarily non-resident, is taxed on in the tax year of return to UK

Income remitted to the UK by non-UK domiciliary while outside the UK

Gains

- If gain/loss arises while non-resident
- On asset acquired before became non-resident
- Gain taxed/loss allowed in tax year of return to UK

Except UK residential property - taxed whilst non-resident

9: The taxation of trusts

Topic List

You must be able to suggest appropriate reasons for adopting a trust tax planning strategy.

You must also be able to calculate the income tax payable by trustees or beneficiaries, including the additional tax charge due from the trustees of a discretionary trust where the tax pool is insufficient to cover the tax credit attached to distributions to beneficiaries.

This chapter also covers the inheritance tax and capital gains tax implications of setting up and using a trust, and the tax implications of assets leaving a trust.

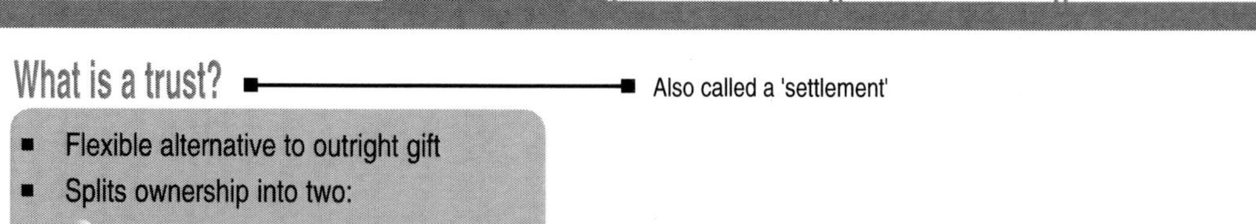

What is a trust?

- Also called a 'settlement'

- Flexible alternative to outright gift
- Splits ownership into two:
  1. Legal ownership – Trustees
     - Trust assets held in trustees' name
  2. Beneficial ownership – Beneficiaries
     - Can benefit from the income and/or capital of the trust assets

Why use a trust?

- Preserve family wealth
- Flexibility over future beneficiaries and destination of property
- Preserving assets for minors
- Concealing ownership

Settlor interested

A trust is 'settlor interested' if the **settlor, spouse/ civil partner** or **unmarried minor child** can potentially benefit from the trust

- Under 18

Unmarried minor child can benefit

- If income paid to or for the benefit of the child, income is treated as settlor's income not the child's
- Exception: if income < £100 pa gross

Offshore trusts

- Gains also taxable on settlor

- UK domiciled settlor → all trust income taxable on settlor
- Non-UK domiciled settlor → UK income and remitted overseas income taxable on settlor

Settlor or spouse/CP can benefit

- Income treated as settlor's income not the trustees'
- Settlor can reclaim tax paid on the trust income from trustees

Capital sums

- Where trustee(s)
  - loan money to settlor/spouse
  - repay loan to settlor/spouse
  - pay money to 3rd party on settlor's behalf
- Settlor is taxed on lower of:
  - capital sum paid
  - trust's available income

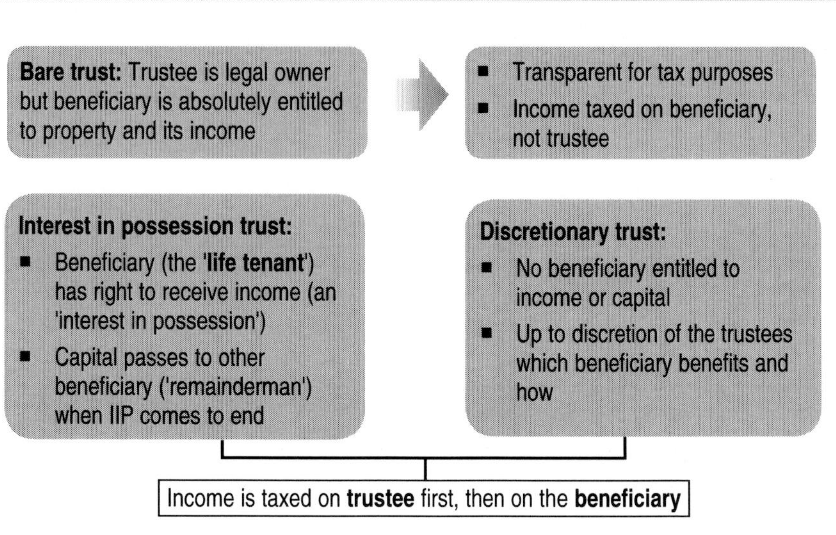
Bare trust: Trustee is legal owner but beneficiary is absolutely entitled to property and its income
- Transparent for tax purposes
- Income taxed on beneficiary, not trustee

Interest in possession trust:
- Beneficiary (the '**life tenant**') has right to receive income (an 'interest in possession')
- Capital passes to other beneficiary ('remainderman') when IIP comes to end

Discretionary trust:
- No beneficiary entitled to income or capital
- Up to discretion of the trustees which beneficiary benefits and how

Income is taxed on **trustee** first, then on the **beneficiary**

IIP trustees

- Calculate income in same way as for an individual eg, property income
- No:
  - Personal allowance
  - Savings nil rate band
  - Dividend nil rate band
  - Bands of income
- No deduction for trust management expenses
- All income taxed at basic rates:
  - Non-savings: 20%
  - Savings: 20%
  - Dividends: 7.5%

Set expenses against dividend income first

IIP beneficiaries (life tenants)

- Entitled to trust's net income (ie, after trust management expenses)
- Receive R185 statement of income showing net amount and tax credit
- Income retains its nature (eg, rental income received by trust is taxed as rental income in beneficiary's hands)
- Taxed at beneficiary's rate(s)

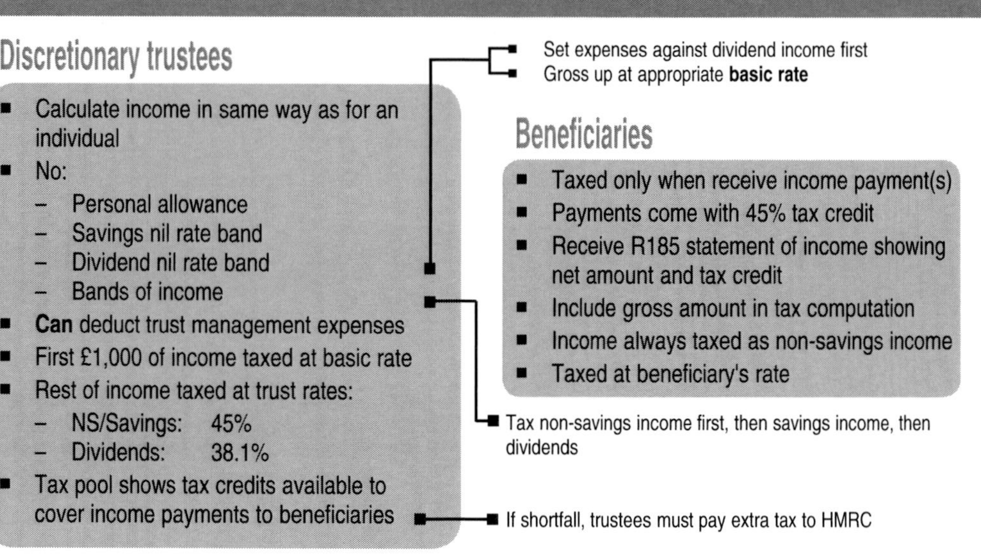

Discretionary trustees

- Calculate income in same way as for an individual
- No:
  - Personal allowance
  - Savings nil rate band
  - Dividend nil rate band
  - Bands of income
- **Can** deduct trust management expenses
  - Set expenses against dividend income first
  - Gross up at appropriate **basic rate**
- First £1,000 of income taxed at basic rate
- Rest of income taxed at trust rates:
  - NS/Savings: 45%
  - Dividends: 38.1%
  - Tax non-savings income first, then savings income, then dividends
- Tax pool shows tax credits available to cover income payments to beneficiaries
  - If shortfall, trustees must pay extra tax to HMRC

Beneficiaries

- Taxed only when receive income payment(s)
- Payments come with 45% tax credit
- Receive R185 statement of income showing net amount and tax credit
- Include gross amount in tax computation
- Income always taxed as non-savings income
- Taxed at beneficiary's rate

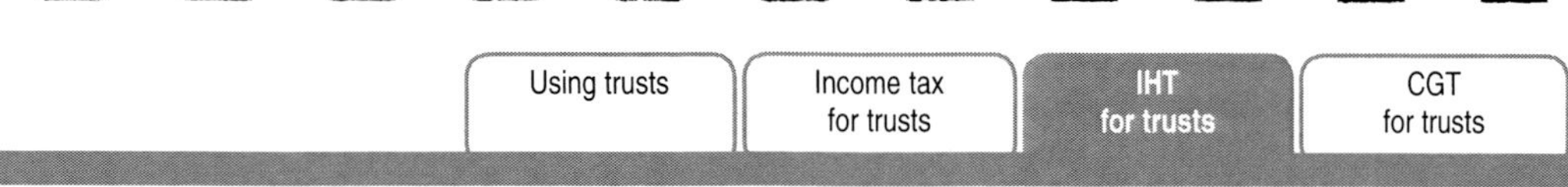

Lifetime trusts

All trusts set up during lifetime are 'relevant property trusts' (RPTs) and suffer the following IHT charges:

1. Exit charge
2. Principal charge

- Exception: Transfer to **bare trust** = PET; transfer from bare trust not a transfer
- Don't forget! There is also a CLT when the trust is set up.

Exit charge

- Charged when assets leave an RPT and pass to a beneficiary

Principal charge (PC)

- Charged every 10 years from date trust set up
- Max 6%

Calculating the exit charge before first principal charge

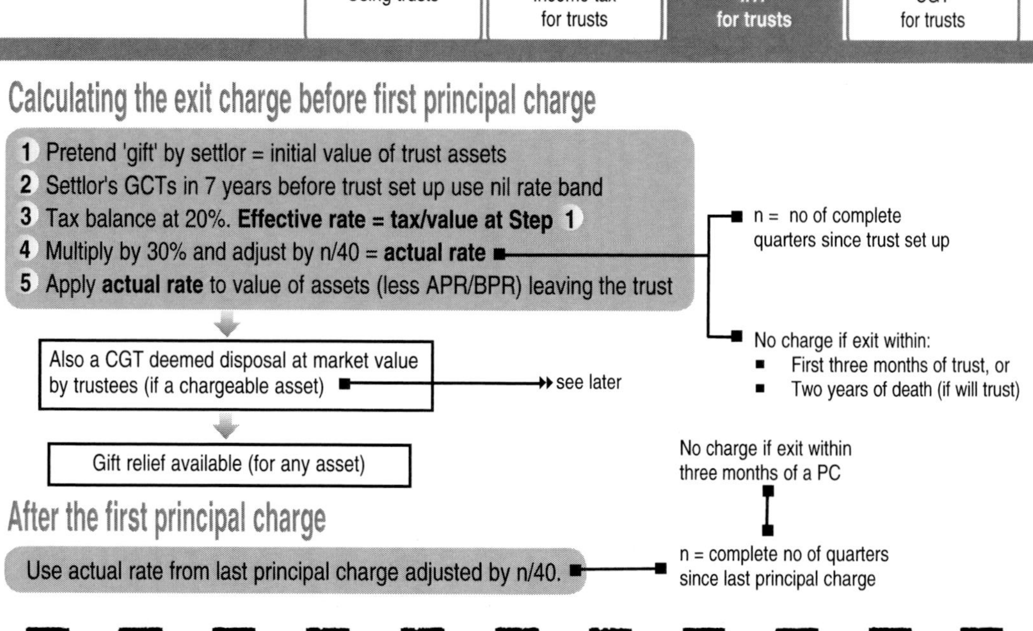

Calculating the principal (10-year) charge

1. Pretend 'gift' by settlor = current value of trust assets (less APR/BPR)
2. Settlor's GCTs in 7 years before trust set up and value of transfers out of trust in previous 10 years use nil rate band
3. Tax balance at 20%. **Effective rate = tax/value at stage 1**
4. Multiply by 30% = **actual rate**
5. Apply **actual rate** to current value of assets

Include undistributed income within the trust for more than 5 years at 10-year anniversary

No CGT

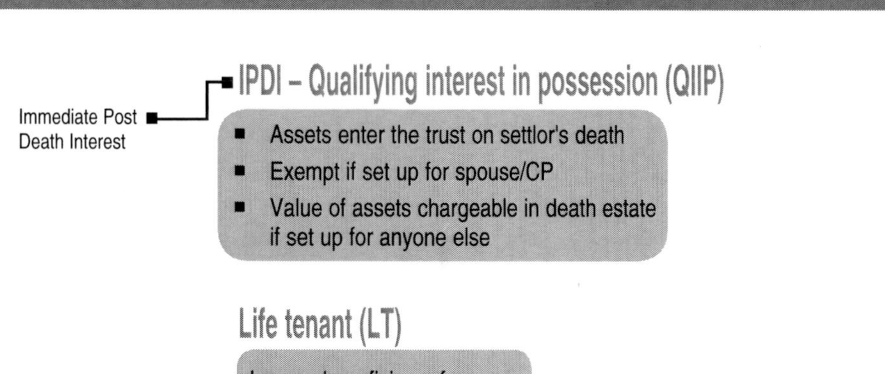

IPDI – Qualifying interest in possession (QIIP)

Immediate Post Death Interest

- Assets enter the trust on settlor's death
- Exempt if set up for spouse/CP
- Value of assets chargeable in death estate if set up for anyone else

Life tenant (LT)

Income beneficiary of an interest in possession trust

QIIP ends during LT's lifetime

Depends who receives the trust assets

Who receives assets

- LT – No transfer of value
- LT's spouse/CP/charity – Exempt
- Any other individual – PET
- Bare trust – PET
- Any other trust – CLT

QIIP ends on LT's death

- Include in LT's death estate as settled property
- Exempt if **remainderman** is spouse/CP
- If chargeable, calculate IHT on combined value of LT's free estate and settled property
  - Tax on free estate paid by executors
  - Tax on settled property paid by QIIP trustees

Remainderman

Capital beneficiary of an interest in possession trust

Remainderman's interest is **excluded property** (ie, outside the scope of IHT)

Exception: Disposals by **bare trustees** is a disposal by the beneficiary

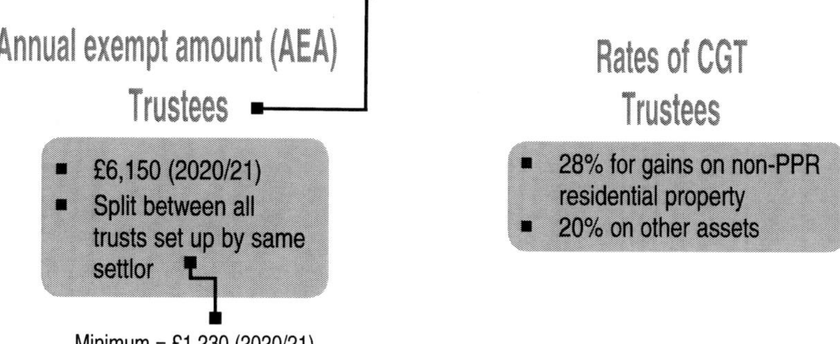

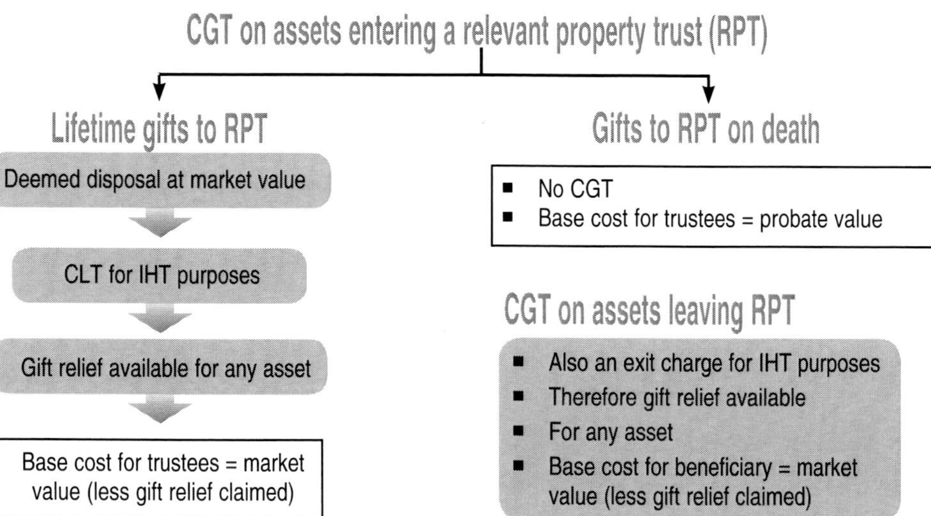

CGT on assets entering a relevant property trust (RPT)
Lifetime gifts to RPT
Deemed disposal at market value
CLT for IHT purposes
Gift relief available for any asset
Base cost for trustees = market value (less gift relief claimed)
Gifts to RPT on death
No CGT
Base cost for trustees = probate value
CGT on assets leaving RPT
Also an exit charge for IHT purposes
Therefore gift relief available
For any asset
Base cost for beneficiary = market value (less gift relief claimed)

CGT on assets entering a QIIP

- No CGT
- Base cost for trustees = probate value

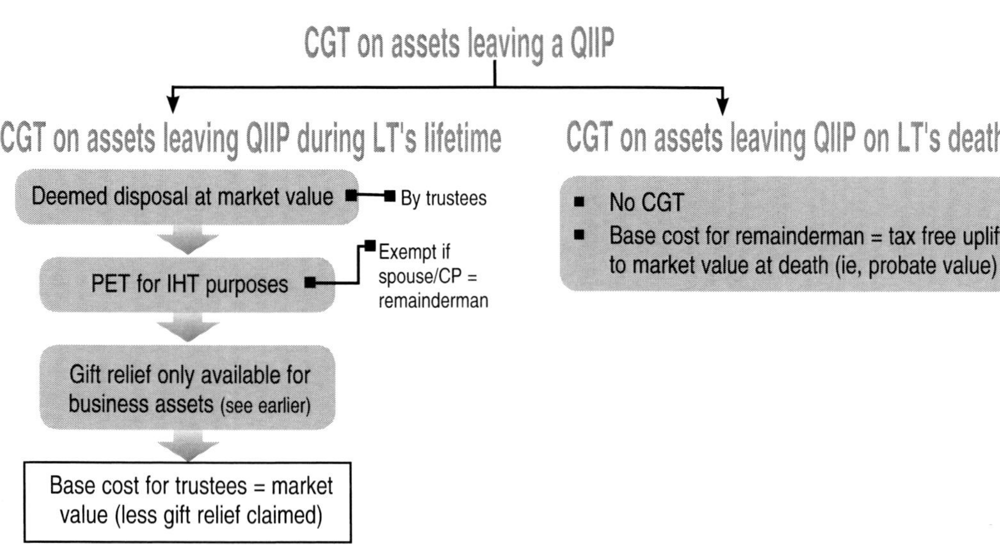

CGT on assets leaving a QIIP
CGT on assets leaving QIIP during LT's lifetime
Deemed disposal at market value
By trustees
PET for IHT purposes
Exempt if spouse/CP = remainderman
Gift relief only available for business assets (see earlier)
Base cost for trustees = market value (less gift relief claimed)
CGT on assets leaving QIIP on LT's death
No CGT
Base cost for remainderman = tax free uplift to market value at death (ie, probate value)

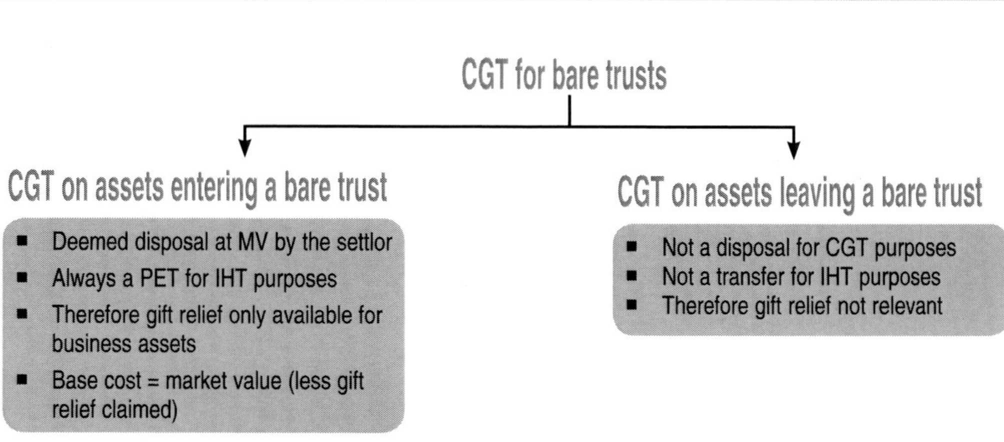
CGT for bare trusts
CGT on assets entering a bare trust
Deemed disposal at MV by the settlor
Always a PET for IHT purposes
Therefore gift relief only available for business assets
Base cost = market value (less gift relief claimed)
CGT on assets leaving a bare trust
Not a disposal for CGT purposes
Not a transfer for IHT purposes
Therefore gift relief not relevant

10: Corporation tax for a single company

Topic List

Corporation tax computation

R&D expenditure

IFAs

Companies with investment business

Substantial shareholding exemption

Some of the topics in this chapter eg, the corporation tax computation and administration, are revision from Tax Compliance.

You must be aware of when an additional deduction may be made for research and development expenditure and when a tax credit may be claimed.

It is essential that you can explain when the disposal of a shareholding is an exempt disposal.

Residence

A UK resident company is chargeable on its worldwide profits. A company is resident in the UK if it is incorporated in the UK or if its central management and control are in the UK.

Alert! An accounting period can never be > 12 months.

If a company prepares accounts for a longer period, it must be split into 2 CT accounting periods.

1st 12 months form the 1st accounting period

Remaining months form the 2nd accounting period

Period of account

A period of account is the period for which accounts are prepared.

Accounting period

An accounting period is the period for which corporation tax is charged.

- Begins when the company starts to trade, acquires a source of income or immediately after the end of the previous accounting period.
- Ends 12 months after it starts, when the period of account ends, when it starts or ceases to trade or when it ceases to be UK resident.

Taxable total profits

A company's **taxable total profits** are arrived at by adding together its various sources of income and chargeable gains and then deducting qualifying donations.

◂ see earlier

Profits of trade net of capital allowances → Trading income

Interest from non-trading loan relationships (eg, bank/building society interest) → Non-trading loan relationships

Any income not otherwise charged → Miscellaneous income

Income from property in the UK → Property income

Donations paid in the accounting period → Qualifying donations

Proforma for calculating taxable total profits

	£
Trading income	X
Non-trading loan relationships	X
Miscellaneous income	X
Property income	X
Chargeable gains	X
Total profits	X
Qualifying donations	(X)
Taxable total profits	X

Alert! Exempt dividends from other UK and overseas companies are not included in taxable total profits.

Corporation tax rate

Rate of corporation tax (CT) is set for financial years

A financial year runs from 1 April in one year to 31 March in the next. **Financial Year 2020 (FY2020) runs from 1 April 2020 to 31 March 2021.**

19% for FY20

19% for FY19

If there is a change in the rate of CT, and a company's accounting period does not fall entirely into one Financial Year, the augmented profits of the period are time apportioned to the two financial years.

Augmented profits (AP)

Taxable total profits plus exempt ABGH distributions — UK and overseas dividends from non-51% subsidiaries

≤ £1.5 million | > £1.5 million | > £20 million

- Multiply by months/12 for short accounting periods
- Share equally between the number of '**related 51% group companies**'

≤ £1.5 million: Payment due date is 9 months + 1 day after end of the accounting period

> £1.5 million / > £20 million: Payment due in instalments unless:

- CT liability < £10,000, or
- Not large in PY, and AP ≤ £10m

Starting in month 7 for > £1.5m
Starting in month 3 for > £20m

Example

A Ltd, which has one related 51% group company, prepares accounts for the nine months to 31.3.21. The limit for this period is:

$$9/12 \times \frac{1{,}500{,}000}{2}$$

= £562,500

Related 51% group company

- Include 51% direct and indirect subsidiaries at the end of the previous accounting period
- Ignore passive companies

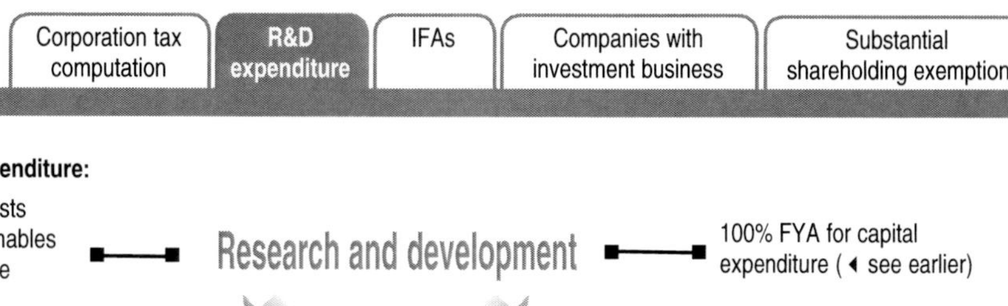

Eligible expenditure:

- Staff costs
- Consumables
- Software

Research and development

100% FYA for capital expenditure (◂ see earlier)

SMEs

- Additional 130% × eligible expenditure
- If company has trading loss can claim tax credit of 14.5% × lower of:
  - The available trading loss; or
  - 230% of R&D expenditure

Large companies

- Elect for R&D expenditure credit (RDEC) at 13% for expenditure incurred on or after 1 April 2020 and 12% for expenditure incurred before 1 April 2020.

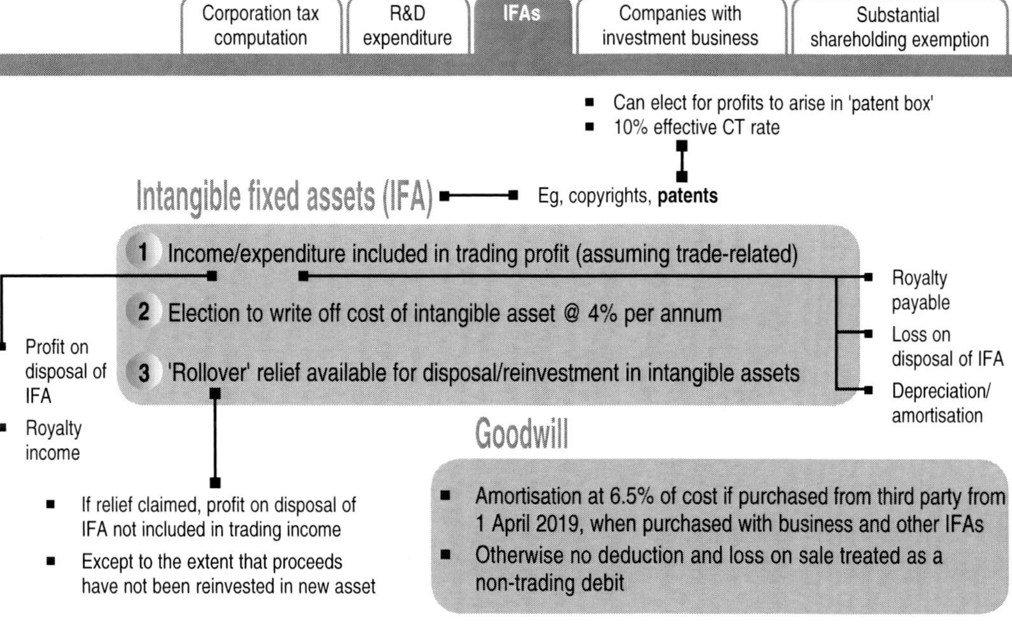

- Can elect for profits to arise in 'patent box'
- 10% effective CT rate

Intangible fixed assets (IFA)
Eg, copyrights, **patents**

1 Income/expenditure included in trading profit (assuming trade-related)
2 Election to write off cost of intangible asset @ 4% per annum
3 'Rollover' relief available for disposal/reinvestment in intangible assets

- Profit on disposal of IFA
- Royalty income

- Royalty payable
- Loss on disposal of IFA
- Depreciation/ amortisation

- If relief claimed, profit on disposal of IFA not included in trading income
- Except to the extent that proceeds have not been reinvested in new asset

Goodwill
- Amortisation at 6.5% of cost if purchased from third party from 1 April 2019, when purchased with business and other IFAs
- Otherwise no deduction and loss on sale treated as a non-trading debit

Patent box – post BEPS

Separate taxable total profits (TTP)

Patent box profits (A)

Separate in to different streams

From each profit stream deduct:

- 10% return on costs
- Marketing royalty

This gives profits (C)

Apply the 'R&D fraction' to profits (C) from each profit stream to give adjusted patent box profits (D)

R&D fraction lower of

- 1; and
- $(D + S_1) \times 1.3 / (D + S_1 + A + S_2)$.

Other trading profits (B)

Corporation tax payable

	£
Total profits (A + B)	x
Less (D) × (19% – 10%)/19%	(x)
Taxable total profits	x
Corporation tax payable @ 19%	x

Companies with investment business

Includes trading companies with shares in subsidiary

Management expenses

- Expenses of management are deductible in computing taxable profits
- Carry forward or group relieve unused expenses of management

Interest on loans to purchase investments are loan relationship debits not management expenses

Changes in ownership

see Chapter 12

- New owner cannot use excess management expenses if reason for sale = to use them
- Management expenses lost if significant increase in company's capital after change

Significant means post-change capital:

- Increases by £1m; and
- Is ≥ 125% of pre-change capital

Losses on share sale

A loss on a sale of subscriber shares in a trading company by an 'investment company' can be relieved against:

- Other income in the AP of the loss; then
- Other income in the previous 12 months.

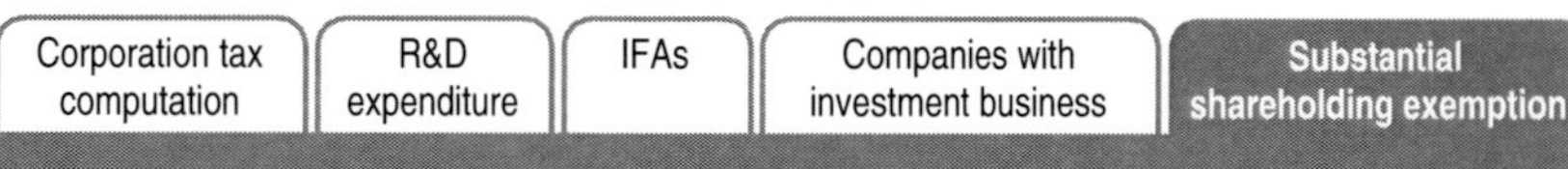

Substantial shareholding exemption

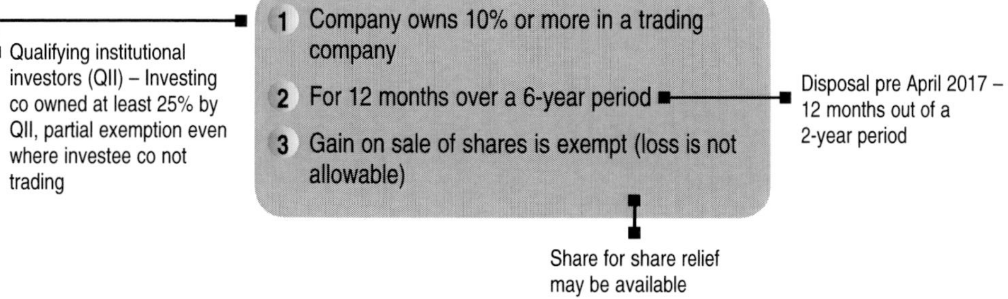

11: Raising finance

Topic List

This chapter explores the more advanced aspects of raising finance including loan relationships, foreign exchange and using leases.

You need to be able to explain the impact, for both the investor and the company, of providing equity finance and/or debt finance.

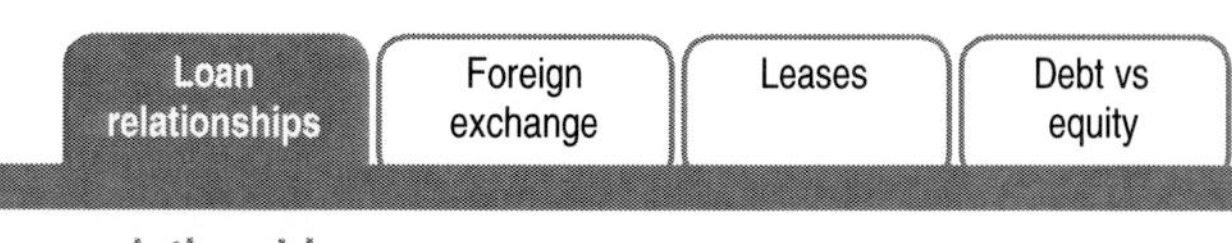

Loan relationships

Subject to corporate interest restrictions ▸▸ see later

Anti-avoidance rules for connected party loans

'Money debt' arising from the lending of money
Rules cover not just interest but expenses, and capital profits and losses on disposal

Trading loan relationship

- Held for trade purposes (eg, debentures issued to acquire plant and machinery)
- Costs (eg, interest accruing) are deductible trading expenses
- Income accruing (eg, interest income) is taxable as trading income

- Usually only banks/financial institutions receive trade related interest income
- However, Interest and FOREX movements in respect of trade debts = trading loan relationships ▸▸ see below

Non-trading loan relationship

- Held for non-trade purposes (eg, debentures issued to buy shares)
- Income accruing taxed as income from non-trading loan relationship
- Deduct expenses accruing from non-trading loan relationship income; a net deficit may arise

Net deficits are relieved as follows:

- Against other profits of same accounting period
- Against non-trading income from loan relationships in previous 12m
- Group relieved
- Carried forward (see Chapter 12)

Non-trading loan relationship

Debits	Credits
Interest payable	Interest receivable
Foreign exchange losses	Foreign exchange gains
Premium on a loan liability	Discount on a loan liability
Incidental costs of loan finance	
Interest on overdue corporation tax	
Impairment loss on an unpaid business payment	

Examples:

- Bringing loan relationship into existence (including abortive costs)
- Making payments under loan relationship/related transaction

Paying interest

Company pays interest net of 20% income tax unless payable:

- To another UK company
- On listed Eurobonds or gilts
- On 'short' loans (not > 12 months), or
- To a non-resident (under double tax treaty)

FOREX gains/losses on:	Tax treatment
Settled trading transactions	Trading income/expense
Monetary items ■ Receivables ■ Payables ■ Overdrafts ■ Loans	■ Loan relationship credit/debit ■ As recorded in the accounts ■ Trading/non-trading as appropriate
Non-monetary items ■ Capital assets	Part of capital profit/loss on sale

- Use sterling, except for ships, aircraft and shares
- For those use tax currency and convert to sterling at date of transaction

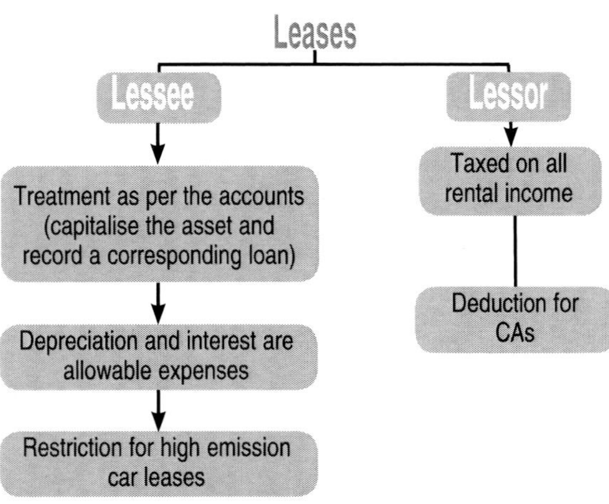
Leases
Lessee
Treatment as per the accounts (capitalise the asset and record a corresponding loan)
Depreciation and interest are allowable expenses
Restriction for high emission car leases
Lessor
Taxed on all rental income
Deduction for CAs

Debt vs equity

	Distribution	Interest
Paying co	Not tax deductible	Tax deductible
Private investor	Taxed at 0%/7.5%/32.5%/38.1%	▪ Taxable at 0%/20%/40%/45%
Corporate investor	▪ Not taxable ▪ May affect augmented profits ▪ SSE for gain?	▪ Taxable loan relationship ▪ Profit/loss also taxable loan relationship

12: Corporation tax losses

Topic List

- Corporate loss relief rules
- Change in ownership
- Choice of loss relief

This chapter begins by recapping the rules on corporation tax losses, and adding additional rules that were not tested at Tax Compliance.

You will be expected to be able to explain loss relief options for trading and non-trading losses available to a company.

You must also be able to calculate the taxable total profits after the losses are relieved and determine when loss relief may be restricted on a change in ownership.

Property losses

- Automatically set off against other profits of the same AP.
- Pre-1 April 2017 excess losses can be:
  - CF as a property loss and offset as far as possible
  - Group relieved
- Post-1 April 2017 excess losses can be:
  - Carried forward as a property loss and set off in part or in whole (by election)
  - Group relieved

Capital losses

- Can only be set against chargeable gains in current or future accounting periods
- Must be set against the first available gains
- Subject to restriction

Non-trading IFA losses

Set off against:

- Total profits of same AP (whole or part of loss)
- Profits of group companies
- CF against future total profits

Trading losses

A company's trading loss may be:

(1) Set against other profits of the **same** accounting period (s.37).

(2) Set against profits of the **previous 12 months** (s.37).

(3) Carried forward (see later).

Before QCDs

If pro-rating is necessary, pro-rate profits before QCDs to compute maximum relief

- If claiming relief (2), must claim relief (1) first.
- Both are all or nothing claims.

Terminal loss relief – last 12 months (s.37)

12 month CB period extended to 36 months where trading loss arose in 12 months before trade ceases.

Carried forward trading losses

Pre-1 April 2017

- Against first future trading profits of the same trade (s45)
- No claim to carry forward or relieve

Post-1 April 2017

- Usually against total profits (whole or part of loss) (S45A)
- No claim to carry forward but claim for amount to relieve (2 years of end of AP)

Terminal loss relief – carried forward losses (s.45F)

Pre-1 April 2017:

- Carry back 3 years from end of terminal period LIFO
- Against trading profits of the same trade

Both:

- But not before 1 April 2017
- Not in period of loss or before period of loss

Post-1 April 2017:

- Carry back 3 years from end of terminal period LIFO
- Usually against total profits

Non-trading loan relationship deficit

Set off against:

- Other profits of same AP
- Non-trading loan relationship income of previous 12 months
- Profits of group companies
- Carried forward

- All or nothing claim if pre-1 April 2017 deficit; any part of the deficit if post-1 April 2017 deficit

- Can make partial claims
- Preserves DTR credits/other CT reliefs

- Pre-1 April 2017 deficit against non-trading profits (incl. gains); post-1 April 2017 deficit against total profits

Restriction on carry forward relief

(offset of profits arising post-1 April 2017 and capital gains arising post-1 April 2020)

Deductions allowance

Maximum deduction =
£5 million + 50% excess profits

- Trading losses
- NTLR deficits
- Property losses
- IFA non-trading losses
- Management expenses
- Capital losses

Profits before deducting:

- c/f losses
- c/b reliefs
- Post-1 April 2017 c/f group relief (see later)

Look separately at relief against:

- Trading profits (eg, pre-1 April 2017 trading losses)
- Non-trading profits (eg, pre-1 April 2017 NTLR deficits)
- Capital gains (e.g. capital losses)
- Total profits (eg, post-1 April 2017 losses/ deficits)

Company can choose how much of the £5 million allowance is allocated to each type of profit or gain

Change in ownership

1 If in any period of three years there is a change in ownership **and** a major change in nature or conduct of trade; or

2 Scale of trading becomes negligible followed by a change in ownership followed by revival of trade.

- Applies if both events within:
  - Three years for pre-1 April 2017 change (either or both)
  - Five years for both changes post-1 April 2017 (not starting more than three years before ownership change)

Restrictions on losses

- Trading losses cannot be carried forward past date of change in ownership
- Trading losses cannot be carried back prior to date of change in ownership
- Shell company cannot carry non-trade debits/deficits on loan relationships or IFAs forwards or back from date of change in ownership
  - Has no trade, investment or UK property business

The choice between reliefs

- Consider timing: earlier relief is better than later relief
- Avoid losing relief for qualifying donations
- Impact on instalment payments

Greater flexibility re: partial claims since 1 April 2017

13: Anti-avoidance for owner-managed businesses

Topic List

Employment vs self-employment

Use of intermediaries

Close companies

Anti-avoidance legislation stops taxpayers using tax laws for unintended purposes.

You need to be able to explain why an individual might prefer to be treated as self-employed rather than employed.

In addition, you must understand when the intermediaries legislation applies and the tax implications for the company and owner.

You also need to be able to identify a close company and explain the tax implications for the company and participators.

Use HMRC guidance to decide if an individual's income should be taxed as employment or trading income.

Employee

Contract of service

- Have to do the work themself
- Someone can tell them what to do, and when and how to do it
- Provided with holiday pay, sick pay or a pension
- Paid hourly/weekly or given number of hours a week or month
- Work wholly or mainly for one business
- Expected to work at the premises of the person they are working for

Self employed

Contract for services

- Responsible for how the business is run
- Risk own capital
- Bear losses as well as taking profits
- Control
- Provide the major items of equipment needed to do job
- Can hire people to do the work
- Have to correct unsatisfactory work in own time and at own expense

Check Employment Status for Tax (CEST) is a useful online tool to help determine status.

Tax consequences	Employed	Self employed
Type of income	Employment income	Trading income
Basis of assessment	Receipts basis	Current year basis, with special rules in opening and closing years
Income assessed	■ Earnings from employment ■ Includes taxable benefits for private use	■ All trading profits ■ Adjust for private use
Allowable expenses	Wholly, exclusively and necessarily incurred in the performance of the duties of the employment	Wholly and exclusively incurred for the purposes of the trade
National insurance contributions	■ Class 1 primary ■ Class 1 secondary ■ Class 1A ■ Class 1B	■ Class 2 ■ Class 4
Payment of income tax and national insurance contributions	Monthly via PAYE system	■ IT and class 4 NICs – self-assessment (POAs and balancing payment)

Personal service companies (IR35)

Individual performs business or domestic services, or acts as an officer, for a client through a UK or offshore intermediary (eg, company) which would be employment if performed direct

'Relevant engagement'

- Deemed employment payment at end of tax year
- Treated as made by intermediary to worker
- Subject to PAYE/NIC

No NIC employment allowance available

Intermediary pays PAYE/NIC (unless working for a public authority)

'Deemed payment' = income received from 'relevant engagement' less:

- 5% flat rate expenses allowance (except when working for a public authority)
- Actual deductible expenses
- Actual salary paid by intermediary to individual
- Employer's NIC on that salary
- Employer pension contributions

Managed service companies

- Supplies individual workers' services to third party clients
- Workers receive majority of payments
- Payments higher than if had been employees

- Non-employment income = earnings
- Deemed employment payment each time actual payment made to workers without deduction of IT/NIC
- Chargeable when made (not end of tax year)
- Can only deduct actual deductible expenses

Close companies

- UK company
- Controlled (> 50%) by 5 or fewer participators (broadly shareholders) or any number of directors → Include associates' interests

1 Loans to participators

- Pay 32.5% of loan to HMRC
- This is repaid by HMRC when the loan is repaid or written off

Also applies if loan made to:

- Trustees – if trust or beneficiary = participator or associate of participator
- LLP/partnership – if partner = participator or associate of participator

Loan repaid

Treat as repayment of new loan if:

- New loan of ≥ £5,000 is taken out within 30 days; or
- Balance before repayment ≥ £15,000 and intend to take new loan

Loan written off

- Treated as a dividend for the individual
- Not deductible for the company

Exclusions

Loans to directors/employees ≤ £15,000 per borrower if:

- The borrower works full-time for the company; and
- Does not have a material interest (> 5%) in the company

2 Benefits given to participators

- If the participator is not an employee, treat the value of benefit (calculated as for earnings) as though it were a distribution
- Disallow the actual cost in computing the company's trading profit

32.5% tax charge if:

- Part of tax avoidance arrangement; and
- No charge would otherwise arise

Qualifying interest

- Interest on loan to purchase shares in close company is deductible
- Subject to cap on income tax reliefs ◄ see earlier

14: Groups and consortia

Topic List

You must be able to identify the companies to which a loss may be surrendered within a group and how much may be surrendered.

In addition, you must be able to determine the optimum loss relief to achieve the group's objectives.

You must also be able to identify a gains group and advise on the ways of reducing chargeable gains within that group.

Group relief group

One company must have a 75% effective interest in the other, or there must be a third company which has a 75% effective interest in both.

- Of share capital **and** income **and** net assets on a winding up.

Group relief

- Restrictions if change in ownership of company

- Current period losses of one group company can be set against total profits of another.
- Post-1 April 2017 carried forward losses can be set against total profits of another company.

- £5m deduction allowance applies to the group as a whole
- Co cannot claim c/f GR if it has unused c/f losses of own, and co cannot surrender c/f losses for GR if it could use them itself

Current year losses available to surrender

- Trading losses
- Excess property business losses
- Excess qualifying charitable donations (QCDs)
- Deficits on non-trading loan relationships
- Excess management expenses

Note: Different rules for capital losses ⏩ see later

Post-1 April 2017 carried forward losses available to surrender

- Trading losses available against total profits
- Non-trading loan relationship deficits
- Non-trading losses on intangible fixed assets
- Property business losses
- Management expenses of an investment business

Claimant company profits

Total profits available to absorb group relief are total profits after deducting:

- QCDs; and
- Current and brought forward losses.

Claim relief within two years of end of AP of loss

- Group relief claim is normally made on the claimant company's tax return.
- Notice of consent must also be given by surrendering company.

Overseas aspects of group relief

- Group relief for overseas PE's losses if:
  - Not relievable overseas
  - No PE exemption election made
  - Not carrying out separate wholly overseas trade
- Non-UK resident company trading through UK PE or with UK land gains or with UK property business, can be part of group if loss not relievable overseas

Overlapping accounting periods

- Strictly a current period relief.
- If APs do not coincide, profits and losses must be time-apportioned.
- Only profits and losses of period of overlap may be matched up.

Group payments arrangements

- Nominated group company pays instalments for all group companies.
- Can include non-instalment paying companies.

Group tax surrenders also possible

Considerations where period falls in FY2020

- Tax rates have limited impact as FY2020 is 19% (previous year also 19%)
- Instalment payment position
- Cash flow

Other considerations

- Pre-1 April 2017 losses are generally less flexible than post-1 April 2017 so use pre-1 April losses first where possible.
- Don't waste DTR ie, leave sufficient taxable profits in charge after group relief to ensure full DTR is available
- Can disclaim CAs to reduce the amount of a loss for a year
  - Disclaimed CY CAs increase future years' CAs
  - Useful where not all the loss can be relieved and would otherwise be carried forward
- When a company is leaving a group, losses cannot be surrendered from the date that 'arrangements' exist
  - On any change in ownership, carried forward losses cannot be group relieved for five years

Consortia

1. If a company is 75% owned by 20 or fewer other companies, each owning at least 5%, losses can be surrendered by that company to the consortium members or vice versa.

2. Maximum surrender to/from any one member limited to:

   Member's % stake × consortium owned co's profit or loss

Group/consortium company

- Consortium company that is also a member of a group.
- Relief available to consortium members assumes loss set first against:
  - Group/consoritum co's other profits
  - Other group companies' profits

Link company

- Company is both:
  - Consortium member; and
  - Member of a group.
- Losses can be surrendered in any order.

Chargeable gains group

- Starts with principal company (must be included).
- Carries on down with 75% ordinary shareholding at each level.
- Effective interest of principal company in subsidiary company > 50%.

Intra-group transfers

No gain/loss arises when asset is transferred within a chargeable gains group.

- Ignore actual proceeds.
- Deemed proceeds are:
  - Original cost; plus
  - Indexation to date of transfer (or up to Dec 2017).
- Deemed proceeds become base cost for transferee company.

Degrouping charge

- Transferee leaves group within six years
- Gain at transfer added to proceeds on sale of shares
  - Unless leaving other than as a result of share sale, then gain is chargeable on the leaving company (eg, shares issued to third party)

Exempt if substantial shareholding exemption available

Election

Can elect to transfer whole/part of chargeable gain/allowable loss to another member

Pre-entry capital losses

- Company with capital losses joins a group
- Use of the capital losses is restricted
  - Assets sold before joining
  - Assets owned when joined
  - Assets acquired for business purposes from non-group companies

SSE for groups

- Investee company must be trading/part of trading group.
- Exemption does not apply to intra-group transfers.
- Can combine group shareholdings.

Ownership period of shares acquired via intra-group transfer = total time owned by group

Transfer of fixed assets to/from trading stock

- Transfer of fixed asset by one group company to another which transfers it to stock:
  - Immediate chargeable gain/allowable loss in recipient company using MV at date of transfer to stock
  - Subsequent increase in value taxed as trading income when stock sold
- Transfer of stock by one group company to another which transfers it to fixed assets:
  - MV of stock assessed on disposing company as trading income

Recipient company can elect for the whole gain to be assessed as trading income on sale of stock.

Rollover relief

Members of a gains group may be treated as a single unit for rollover relief purposes.

Intangible fixed assets (IFA): group provisions

- Group definition as for chargeable gains groups
- Intra-group transfer is tax neutral
- Group rollover relief available
- No IFA degrouping charge if due to an SSE share disposal

Planning

Minimise group tax payable by transferring gain to company with capital losses.

- Subject to restriction against gains incurred on or after 1 April 2020.

Succession to trade

Not a cessation if trade transferred to company with substantially the same 75% ownership

Tax consequences

- AP ends
- Predecessor can claim CAs
- Successor takes over TWDV
- Successor can use CF losses
  - Losses may be restricted by excess of relevant liabilities over relevant assets

15: International expansion

Topic List

- Company residence
- Non-UK resident companies
- Company migration
- Establishing an overseas business
- Double taxation relief
- OECD Model Convention

You must be able to identify whether a company is UK resident and advise on, and calculate, the UK taxation liabilities of non-UK resident companies.

Advising companies on the implications of migrating overseas is key, along with the alternative methods of establishing a business overseas.

You must be able to calculate DTR and advise on how losses and qualifying charitable donations should be used where DTR is available within a group.

You must also be aware of the implications of the OECD Model Tax Convention.

Residence

A company is resident in the UK if it is:

(1) Incorporated in the UK; or

(2) Its central management and control are in the UK.

A UK resident company is subject to corporation tax on its **worldwide** profits.

Non-UK resident

A non-UK resident company is subject to corporation tax only if:

- Trades through UK **permanent establishment** (PE)
- Has profits of dealing in/developing **or investing in** land **or property** in the UK.
- Has gains on UK land/ UK property rich assets

e-Commerce and PEs

	Website software/ data location	Server equipment location
OECD model agreement	Not PE	Could be PE
UK	Not PE	Not PE

Company residence | **Non-UK resident companies** | Company migration | Establishing an overseas business | Double taxation relief | OECD Model Convention

Non-UK resident companies

- Chargeable to UK CT if carrying on trade in UK through UK 'permanent establishment' (PE); or
- On profits of dealing in/developing **or investing in** land **or property** in the UK.

Usually taxed at main rate on PE's:

- Trading income
- Property income
- Chargeable gains

Eg, branch, office, factory, agent

Chargeable gains

If company trades through (PE), gains on disposals of **UK assets** = taxable in UK

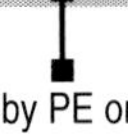

Held by PE or used in trade

Immediate charge if:

- Non-UK company ceases trading through the UK PE
- Non-UK company exports chargeable asset

Gains on UK land/ UK property rich assets

UK residential property

CT on gains post- 5 April 2015 (using MV at 5/4/2015)

UK non-residential property/ UK property rich assets

CT on gains post-5 April 2019 (using MV at 5/4/2019)

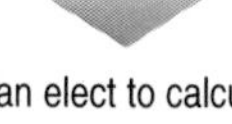

Shares with 75% of assets being UK land (at least 25% holding)

Can elect to calculate the gain based on original cost (in both cases).

Or, for residential only, can elect to use original cost and then time apportion to get post 5 April 2015 part

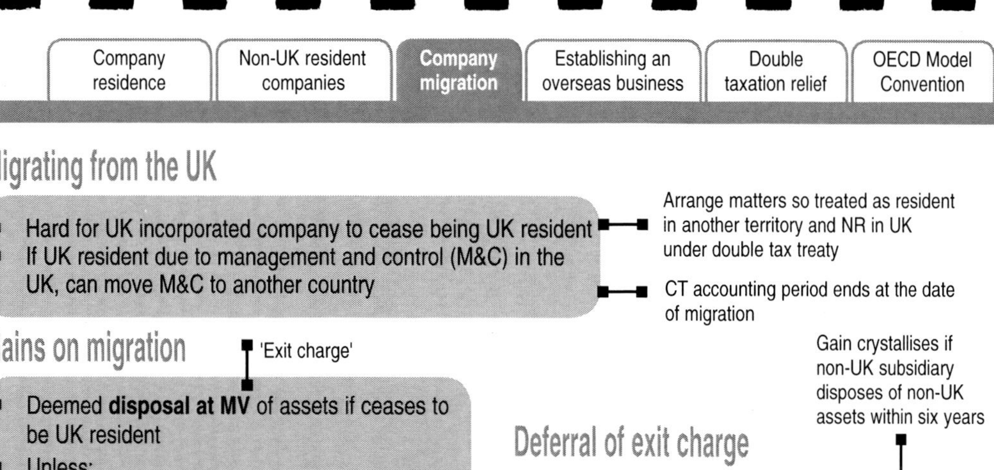

Migrating from the UK

- Hard for UK incorporated company to cease being UK resident
- If UK resident due to management and control (M&C) in the UK, can move M&C to another country

Arrange matters so treated as resident in another territory and NR in UK under double tax treaty

CT accounting period ends at the date of migration

Gains on migration

'Exit charge'

- Deemed **disposal at MV** of assets if ceases to be UK resident
- Unless:
  - Asset in UK; and
  - Used in UK PE.

Gain on these UK assets if:

- Sold
- PE trade ceases
- Assets leave UK

Deferral of exit charge

Can elect to defer gain if 75% non-UK subsidiary for migrations before 1.1.20.

Gain crystallises if non-UK subsidiary disposes of non-UK assets within six years

Choice of overseas entity

	Overseas PE	Overseas subsidiary
Legal status	Single entity (ie, part of UK co)	Separate legal entity
Additional related 51% group company?	No	Yes
Income taxed in the UK company	■ PE's profits = part of trading profits ■ Unless make exemption election	Dividends not usually taxable
Basis of assessment	Arising (accruals) basis	Remittance basis (if divs taxable)
Profits taxed overseas	Yes – DTR available in UK	Yes – DTR available in UK
Overseas trading losses	■ Set against UK co's profits (unless makes exemption election) ■ If separate wholly overseas trade, only set against PE's future trade profits	■ Cannot surrender overseas loss to UK co
UK CAs	Available unless exemption election made	Not available
Transfer of assets to the foreign entity	■ No gains/losses ■ No balancing adjustments	■ Gain/losses ■ Balancing adjustments ■ Incorporation relief may be available

Incorporating an overseas PE

Implications

- PE ceases to trade (when net assets transferred to new overseas company)
- Balancing adjustments on PE assets transferred (in hands of UK company)
- Chargeable gains and losses (in UK company) on disposal of PE assets to overseas

Incorporation relief for gains

Gains can be postponed if

- All PE assets (except cash) are transferred to the overseas company
- Consideration is wholly/ mainly shares (full postponement if all consideration is shares)
- The UK company owns at least 25% of the new overseas company
- A claim is made

Gains crystallise if:

- An asset is sold within six years of transfer
(Gain = remaining deferred gain × Gain on this asset on inc/ Gross gains on inc)
- The shares in the overseas company are sold

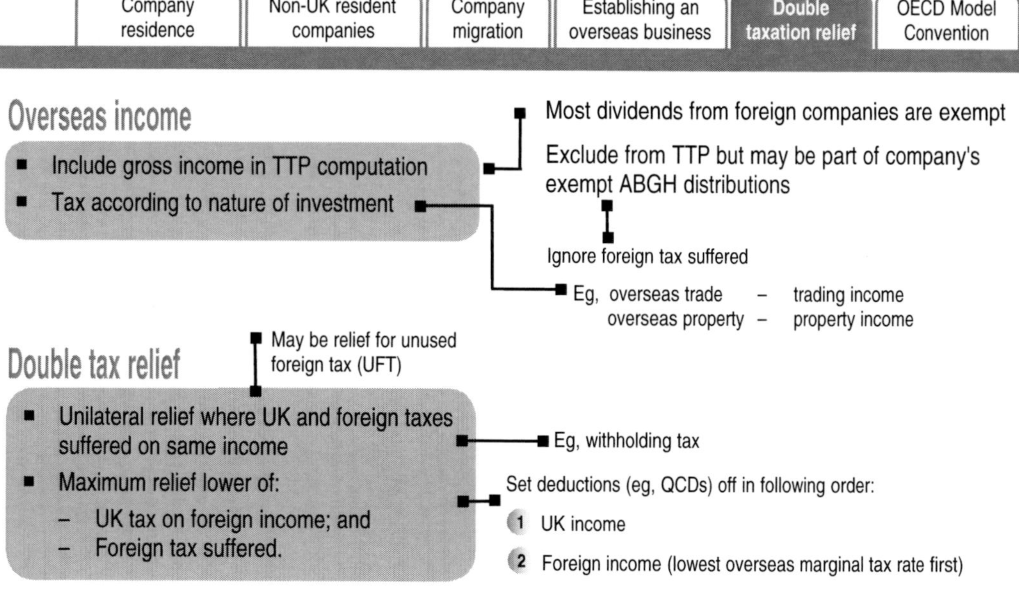
Overseas income
Include gross income in TTP computation
Tax according to nature of investment
Most dividends from foreign companies are exempt
Exclude from TTP but may be part of company's exempt ABGH distributions
Ignore foreign tax suffered
Eg, overseas trade – trading income
overseas property – property income
Double tax relief
May be relief for unused foreign tax (UFT)
Unilateral relief where UK and foreign taxes suffered on same income
Maximum relief lower of:
– UK tax on foreign income; and
– Foreign tax suffered.
Eg, withholding tax
Set deductions (eg, QCDs) off in following order:
1 UK income
2 Foreign income (lowest overseas marginal tax rate first)

OECD model convention

Residence

Resident if liable to tax by reason of its place of management or any other criterion of similar nature

- Tie breaker clause – effective management & control

DTR

Treaty exemption;

or

Credit relief

Business profits of NR company

Only taxed in UK if UK PE

Max w'holding tax:

- Divis $\geq$ 25% = 5%
- Divis <25% = 15%
- Interest = 10%

Permanent establishment

Fixed place of business through which business of an enterprise is carried on

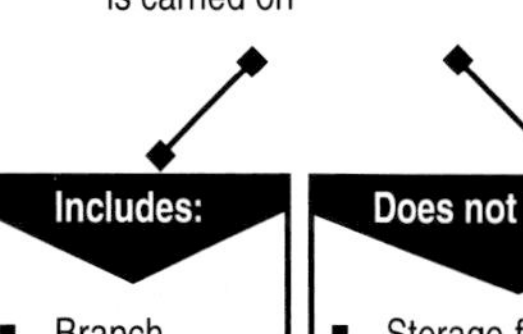

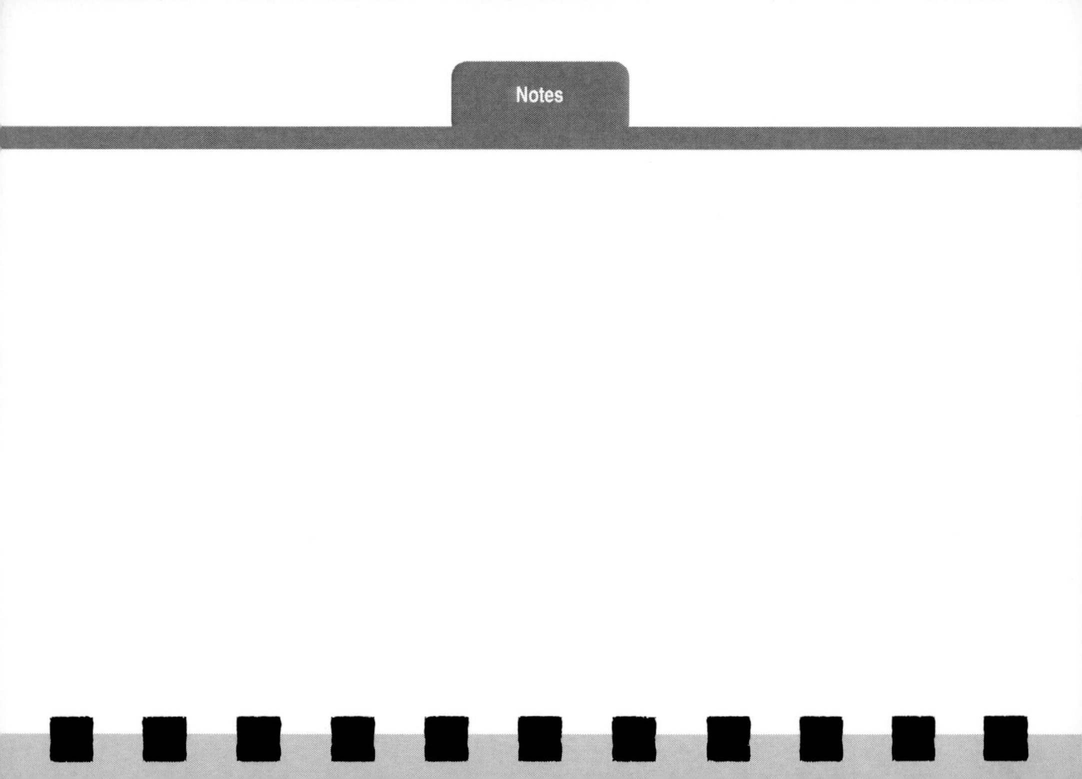
Notes

16: Corporate anti-avoidance

Topic List

You must be able to identify and explain the tax implications arising in connection with:

- *Transactions that fall within the value shifting and depreciatory transaction provisions.*
- *CFC companies and the CFC charge.*
- *Transfer pricing and thin capitalisation rules.*
- *The diverted profits tax rules.*
- *The corporate interest restriction rules.*

Pre-sale dividends

'Dividend stripping'

Cannot use to convert chargeable gains into exempt income

Depreciatory transactions

Capital loss must be reduced to level of true commercial loss

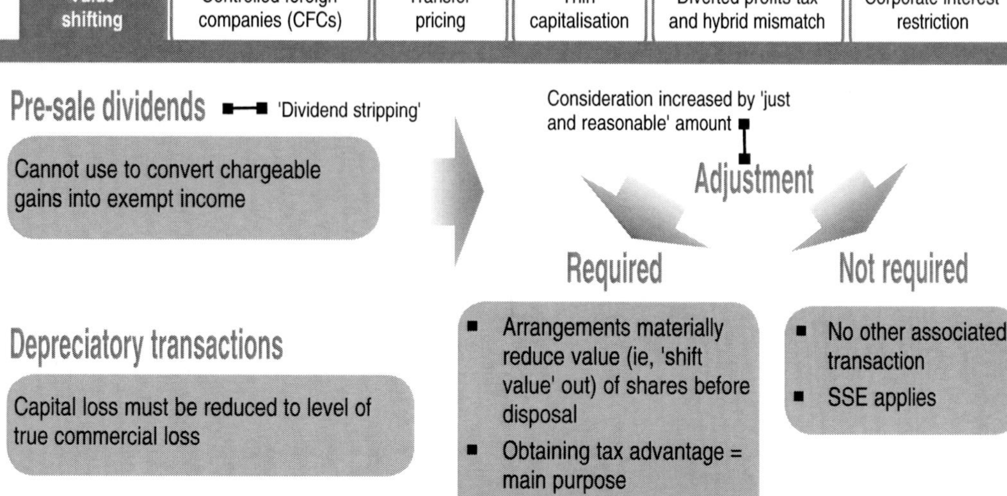

Controlled foreign company (CFC)

Non-UK resident company under UK control if:

- Controlled (> 50%) by UK resident persons; or
- Controlled ≥ 40% by UK and between 40% and 55% by non-UK resident persons; or
- A UK resident company (+ associates) has > 50% investment.

Exemptions

- Exempt period
- Excluded territories
- Low profits exemption
- Low profit margin exemption
- Tax exemption

Tax rate ≥ 75% of UK CT that would have been payable if UK resident

CFC charge

Applies where:

- No exemptions apply;
- There are **chargeable profits**; and
- UK company holds ≥ 25%.

Ie, that pass through the CFC charge 'gateway'

Company must self assess CFC charge at main rate

May be reduced by creditable tax but not by UK losses or surplus expenses

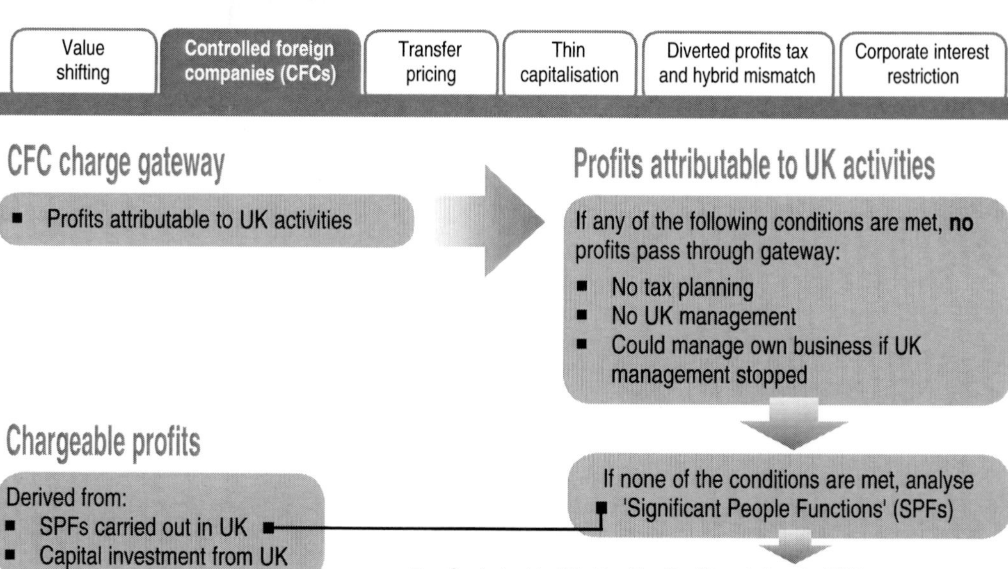
CFC charge gateway
Profits attributable to UK activities
Profits attributable to UK activities
If any of the following conditions are met, no profits pass through gateway:
No tax planning
No UK management
Could manage own business if UK management stopped
If none of the conditions are met, analyse 'Significant People Functions' (SPFs)
Carried out in UK
By connected person
Profits relating to SPFs pass through gateway
Become chargeable profits
Chargeable profits
Derived from:
SPFs carried out in UK
Capital investment from UK

Transfer pricing

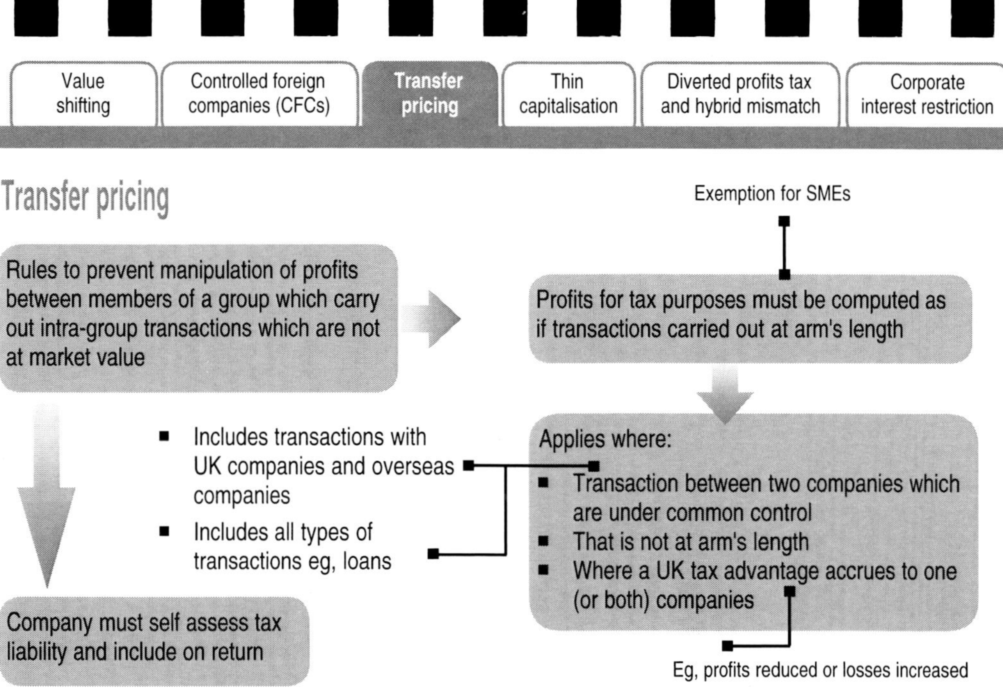

Thin capitalisation

Rules apply where connected company provides loan finance at higher level of debt than a commercial bank would be prepared to lend

Interest disallowed where:

- Excessive loan
- Excessive rate of interest

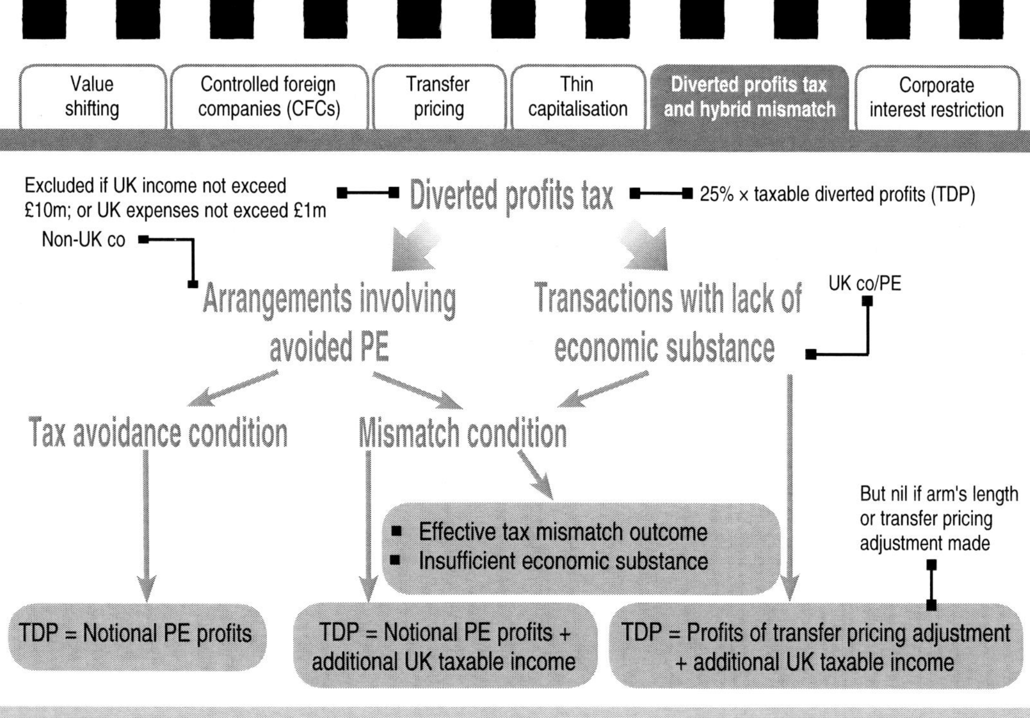
Excluded if UK income not exceed £10m; or UK expenses not exceed £1m
Diverted profits tax
25% × taxable diverted profits (TDP)
Non-UK co
Arrangements involving avoided PE
Transactions with lack of economic substance
UK co/PE
Tax avoidance condition
Mismatch condition
Effective tax mismatch outcome
Insufficient economic substance
But nil if arm's length or transfer pricing adjustment made
TDP = Notional PE profits
TDP = Notional PE profits + additional UK taxable income
TDP = Profits of transfer pricing adjustment + additional UK taxable income

Hybrid mismatch rules

Deny:

- Multiple deduction for same expense
- Deduction to payee without taxation of payee

Examples

- **Financial instruments** allowing deduction of payment as interest but payee treats as exempt dividend
- **Dual residence companies** obtaining expense deduction in both countries
- **PEs** recognised in only one country

Corporate interest restriction

Restriction applies if group aggregate net tax-interest expense exceeds £2 million

Interest capacity

- Current accounting period interest allowance, plus
- Brought forward unused interest allowance (available for 5 years)
- Two methods for calculating interest allowance

Fixed ratio method (Default)

Lower of
- 30% of aggregate tax – EBITDA of group
- 'fixed ratio debt cap'

EBITDA
Earnings before interest, tax, depreciation and amortisation

Fixed ratio debt cap
Net interest expense

Group ratio method (by election)

Lower of
- 'group ratio %' of aggregate tax- EBITDA of group
- 'group ratio debt cap'

Group ratio %
Net group interest expense / Group EDITDA as a percentage

Group ratio debt cap
Net group interest expense

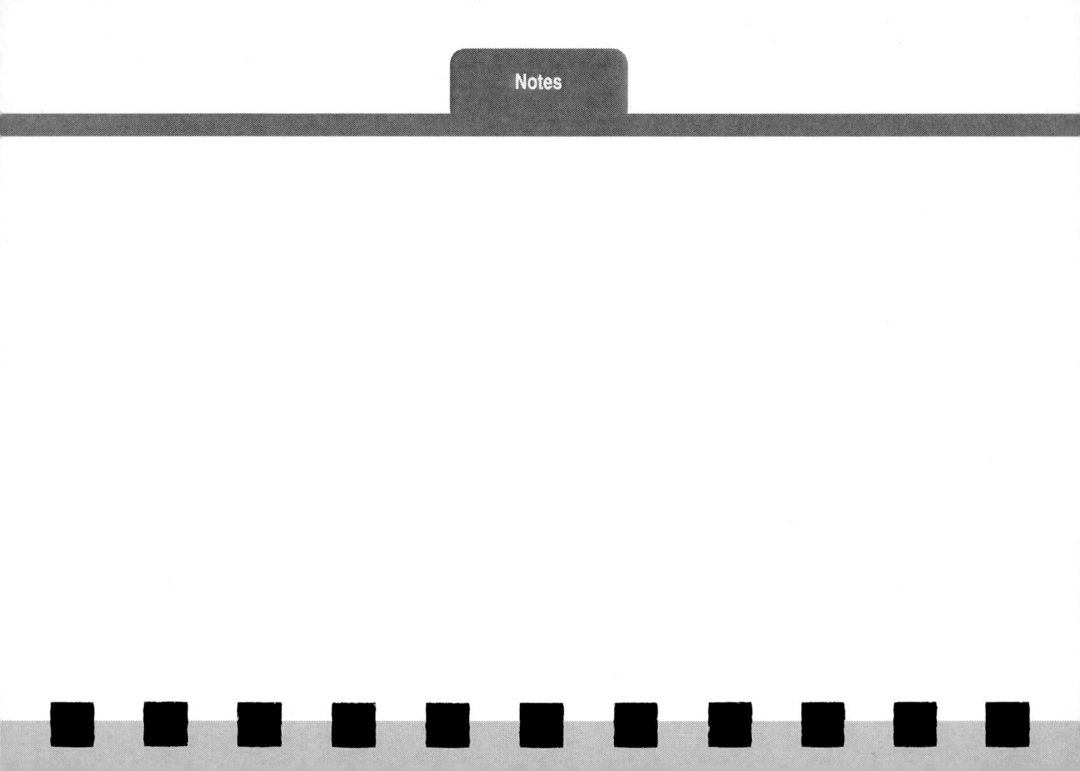
Notes

17: Companies – special situations

Topic List

Company purchase of own shares

Tax implications of administration or liquidation

Tax planning when winding up a company

You must be able to advise on the correct treatment, and calculate the tax liabilities arising as a result, of a company purchase of its own shares from the shareholders.

You must also be able to give appropriate advice, and calculate the tax liabilities arising, in connection with a liquidation or winding up of a company.

Purchase of own shares

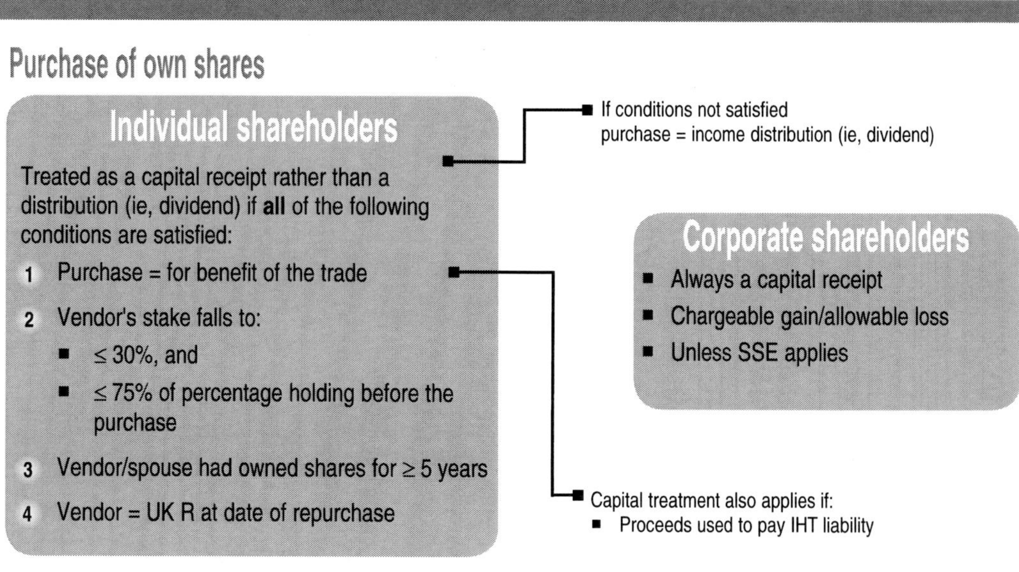

Individual shareholders

Treated as a capital receipt rather than a distribution (ie, dividend) if **all** of the following conditions are satisfied:

1. Purchase = for benefit of the trade
2. Vendor's stake falls to:
   - $\leq$ 30%, and
   - $\leq$ 75% of percentage holding before the purchase
3. Vendor/spouse had owned shares for $\geq$ 5 years
4. Vendor = UK R at date of repurchase

- If conditions not satisfied purchase = income distribution (ie, dividend)
- Capital treatment also applies if:
  - Proceeds used to pay IHT liability

Corporate shareholders

- Always a capital receipt
- Chargeable gain/allowable loss
- Unless SSE applies

Tax implications of administration

New accounting period begins when the company:

- Goes into administration
- Reaches its normal accounting date
- Ceases to be in administration
- Moves out of liquidation into administration (overrides rules on winding up)

- No other CT consequences

Tax implications of liquidation

From the date winding up begins:

- Liquidator pays all CT liabilities arising
- No restriction on c/f capital losses on insolvent liquidation
- AP ends on anniversary of winding up beginning
- Liquidator = beneficial owner of assets
- Final distribution has IT, CGT and CT implications

Tax planning on winding up

Losses

- Cannot CF trading losses so set CY losses against total profits
- Redundancy costs increase CY loss
- Terminal loss relief available
- Terminal loss relief may be available for some c/f losses
- Only losses to date winding up started can be group relieved

Groups

Liquidation of holding co

- Group relief not available
- Gains group continues

Liquidation of subsidiary

- In group relief and gains group until final dissolution

Distribution of assets

For solvent liquidations

- Pre-commencement distributions = dividends
- Post-commencement distributions = capital
  - Part disposal by shareholder

Striking off:

Capital treatment only if distribution < £25,000

18: VAT

Topic List

You must be able to advise on:

- *The correct treatment of and calculate the tax liabilities arising as a result of the acquisition, intra-group transfer, or disposal of property;*
- *The application of the transfer of a going concern rules;*
- *The interaction of the transfer of a going concern, option to tax and capital goods scheme rules; and*
- *The VAT implications of international trade.*

1 Zero rated supplies

Taxable at 0%
Eg, food, books and newspapers

2 Exempt supplies

Not taxable
Eg, insurance, education and health services

3 Standard rated supplies

Taxable at 20%
All supplies which are not zero rated, reduced rate or exempt

4 Reduced rate supplies

Taxable at 5%
Eg, fuel for domestic use, smoking cessation products and contraceptives

Alert! A person making only exempt supplies cannot recover VAT on inputs.
Contrast this with a person making zero rated (taxable supplies) who can recover VAT on inputs.

Land and buildings

1. Land – exempt
2. **New** residential dwellings – zero rated
3. Non-residential converted to residential – zero rated
4. Freehold **new** commercial buildings – standard rated
5. Other sales, leases – exempt

Less than three years old

Subject to landlord's **option to tax** (**not** residential property)

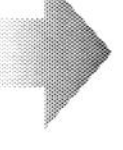

Option to tax

Advantage

☑ VAT-registered landlords can reclaim input VAT

Disadvantages

☒ Must charge VAT on rent

☒ Expensive for non-registered tenants

Capital goods scheme

Initial recovery of input tax on **certain capital goods** is adjusted to reflect variations in the taxable use of those goods.

Applies to:

- **Land and buildings** costing £250,000 or more – adjusted over 10 years
- **Computers** costing £50,000 or more – adjusted over 5 years
- **Boats or aircraft** costing £50,000 or more – adjusted over 5 years

Adjustment each year:

- Difference between taxable use percentage for first year and taxable use percentage for current year
- × 1/10 (land) or 1/5 (computers, boats and aircraft)

On sale:

- Normal annual adjustment, **plus**
- Further adjustment for remaining years assuming taxable use of 0% (exempt sale) or 100% (taxable sale)

Group registration

- Available to companies under **common control**, or where a UK individual/partnership controls a company

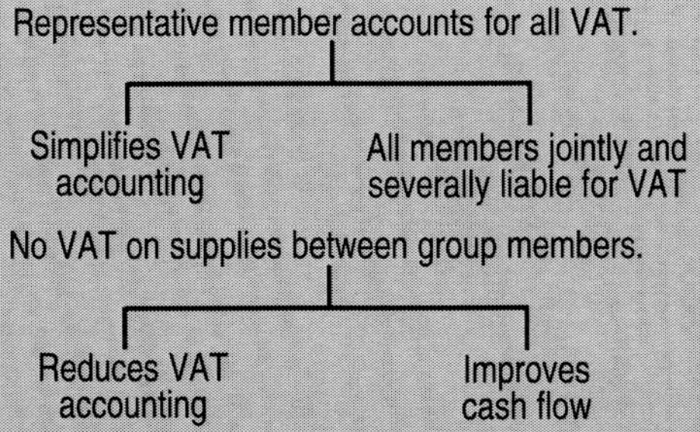

Representative member accounts for all VAT.

- Simplifies VAT accounting
- All members jointly and severally liable for VAT

No VAT on supplies between group members.

- Reduces VAT accounting
- Improves cash flow

- Companies only included in group if specific application made – not automatic
- Consider excluding companies making largely zero rated supplies which could claim monthly VAT repayments

Transfer of a going concern

On a transfer of a whole business (or part that can be run on its own) there is no supply.

SI 1995/1268

Excludes 'taxable land' **unless** transferee opts to tax

Conditions

- The assets must be used by the transferee in carrying on the same kind of business.
- If transferor is registered the transferee must be registered/become liable to be registered following the transfer.
- If only part transferred it must be capable of 'separate operation'.
- There must not be a 'significant' break in trading.

Effect

1 Non-supply

- Transferor must not charge output VAT.
- If output VAT is charged, transferee cannot reclaim as input VAT.
- Any input VAT incurred by the transferor is not directly attributable to a supply for partial exemption purposes.

2 If transferor is registered, transferee must include transferor's past turnover in determining if he is liable to register.

3 Can transfer VAT registration number to new owner. If so, transfers liability for past errors.

Inside the EU

Transactions between the UK and EU countries will not be examined during 2021.

Supply of services

Takes place where:

- Supplier is, if customer not a relevant business person (B2C)
- Customer is, if customer is a relevant business person (B2B)

Reverse charge system if customer is UK VAT registered trader

Outside the EU

Exports

Exports of goods to outside the EU are zero rated.

Imports

Imports of goods from outside the EU are subject to VAT at the same rate as on a sale within the UK, at the point of entry into the UK.

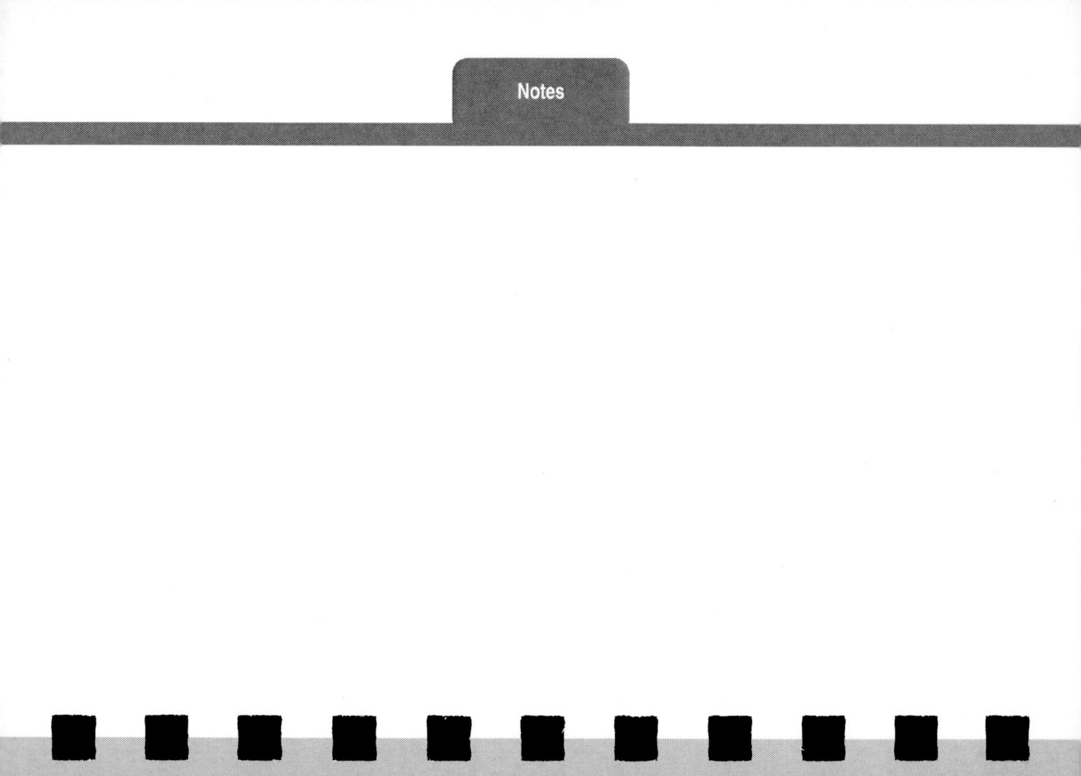
Notes

19: Stamp taxes

Topic List

- Stamp duty
- Stamp duty reserve tax
- Stamp duty land tax
- Stamp duty on incorporation or liquidation
- High value properties

This chapter revises the scope of the different stamp taxes that you saw in the Tax Compliance exam and covers the calculation of the relevant charges and the available exemptions.

You must now also be aware of the stamp duty impact on a corporate transformation, such as incorporation or liquidation.

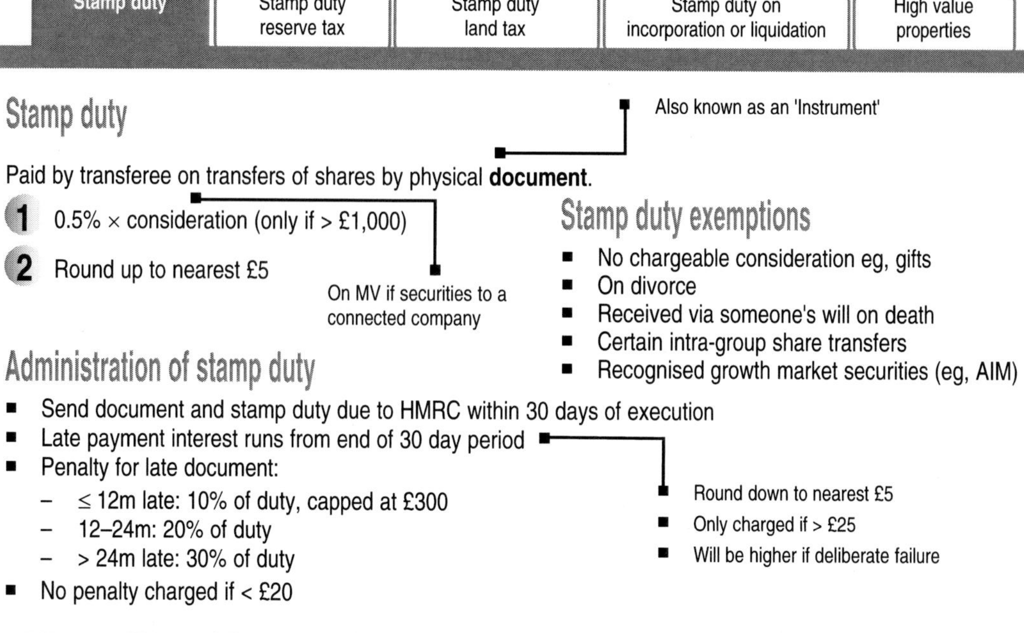

Stamp duty

Paid by transferee on transfers of shares by physical **document**.

Also known as an 'Instrument'

1. 0.5% × consideration (only if > £1,000)
2. Round up to nearest £5

On MV if securities to a connected company

Stamp duty exemptions

- No chargeable consideration eg, gifts
- On divorce
- Received via someone's will on death
- Certain intra-group share transfers
- Recognised growth market securities (eg, AIM)

Administration of stamp duty

- Send document and stamp duty due to HMRC within 30 days of execution
- Late payment interest runs from end of 30 day period
- Penalty for late document:
  - ≤ 12m late: 10% of duty, capped at £300
  - 12–24m: 20% of duty
  - > 24m late: 30% of duty
- No penalty charged if < £20

- Round down to nearest £5
- Only charged if > £25
- Will be higher if deliberate failure

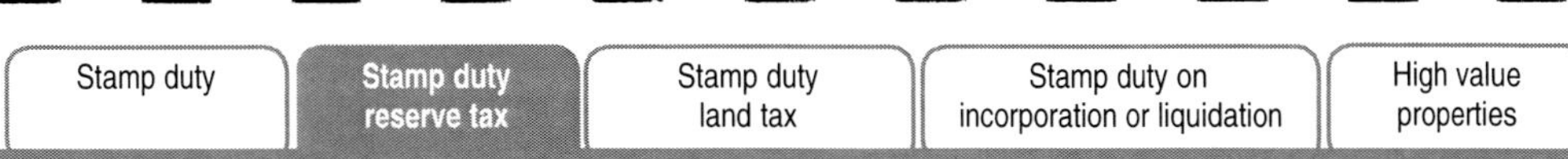

Stamp duty reserve tax

No charge if no consideration (unless transfer of listed securities to connected company – then use MV)

Paid on transfers of shares not caught by stamp duty ie, paperless transactions

1. 0.5% × consideration
2. Do not round

Administration of SDRT

- Collected automatically via stockbrokers
- Due on:
  - 7th day of month following month of contract
  - 14 calendar days after trade date if can be made by CREST

SDRT exemptions

- No chargeable consideration eg, gifts
- On divorce
- Received via someone's will on death
- Certain intra-group share transfers
- Recognised growth market securities (eg, AIM)

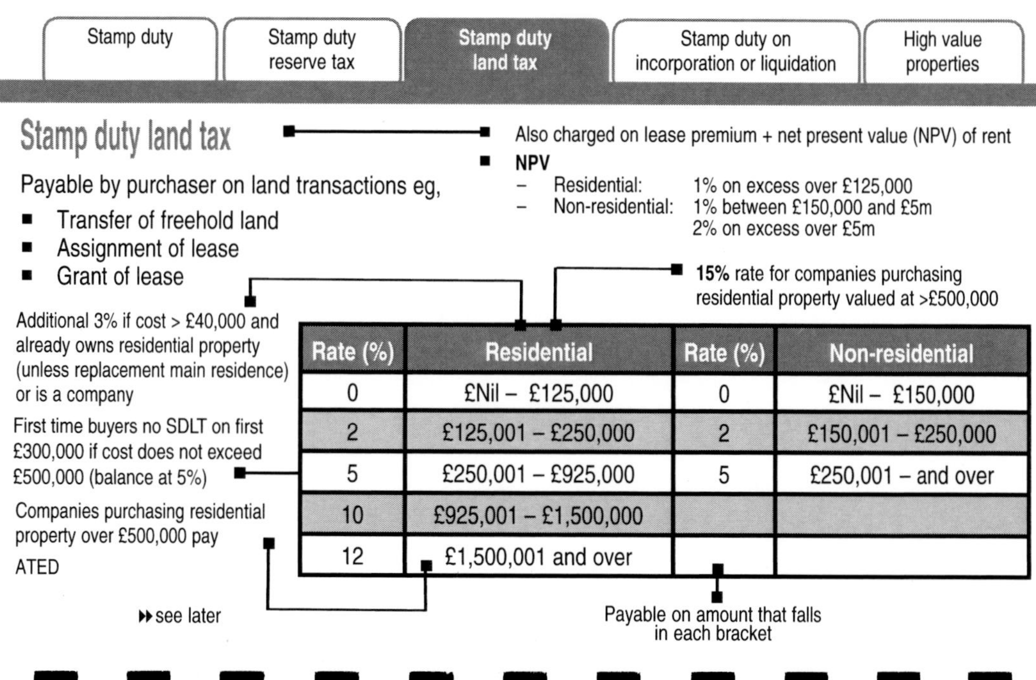

Stamp duty land tax

Also charged on lease premium + net present value (NPV) of rent

- **NPV**
  - Residential: 1% on excess over £125,000
  - Non-residential: 1% between £150,000 and £5m; 2% on excess over £5m

Payable by purchaser on land transactions eg,

- Transfer of freehold land
- Assignment of lease
- Grant of lease

Additional 3% if cost > £40,000 and already owns residential property (unless replacement main residence) or is a company

15% rate for companies purchasing residential property valued at >£500,000

Rate (%)	Residential	Rate (%)	Non-residential
0	£Nil – £125,000	0	£Nil – £150,000
2	£125,001 – £250,000	2	£150,001 – £250,000
5	£250,001 – £925,000	5	£250,001 – and over
10	£925,001 – £1,500,000		
12	£1,500,001 and over		

First time buyers no SDLT on first £300,000 if cost does not exceed £500,000 (balance at 5%)

Companies purchasing residential property over £500,000 pay ATED

▸▸see later

Payable on amount that falls in each bracket

SDLT exemptions

- No chargeable consideration eg, gifts
- On divorce
- Received via someone's will on death
- Transfer of land between members of 75% group

Unless:

- Arrangements
- Not for *bona fide* tax purposes
- Retrospective SDLT if leave group within three years of transfer

SDLT administration

- File land transaction return (even if no SDLT payable)
- Within 14 days of transaction
- Also pay tax within 14 days of transaction
- Late payment interest from end of 14 day period to day before SDLT paid
- Penalties for late filing:
  - Up to three months late: £100 automatic penalty
  - Over three months late: £200 automatic penalty
  - Over one year late: tax geared penalty up to amount of SDLT payable

Company transformations

- **Incorporation** ⏩ see Chapter 23
  - SDLT payable on total value of all land transferred
  - If TOGC, calculate on VAT-exclusive value only
  - No SD on shares received by sole trader as new issue
- **Liquidation** ⏩ see Chapter 17
  - Exempt from SDLT if transferred to shareholder
  - Unless consideration given

Annual tax on enveloped dwellings (ATED)

Annual tax on corporate owners of residential dwellings worth > £500,000

Property value	Annual charge
Up to £500,000	N/A
£500,001 – £1,000,000	£3,700
£1,000,001 – £2,000,000	£7,500
£2,000,001 – £5,000,000	£25,200
£5,000,001 – £10,000,000	£58,850
£10,000,001 – £20,000,000	£118,050
£20,000,001 or more	£236,250

Reliefs

- Properties part of a property rental business
- Property developers and traders
- Certain unoccupied properties

Administration

- Return and payment within 30 days of start of FY/purchase
- Penalties for errors in return, late returns and late
- ATED payment

Use relief declaration return if relief available

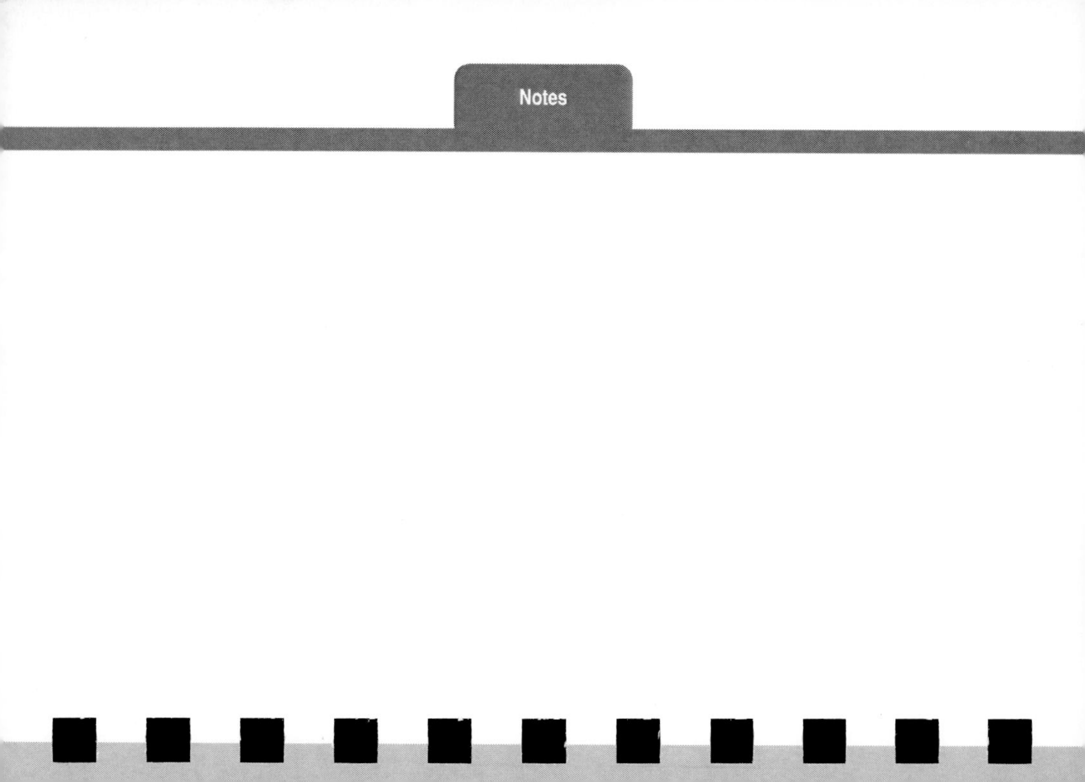

Notes

20: Communication skills

Topic List

- Scenario questions
- Formatting your answer
- Use of legislation

In the exam you will be faced with questions based upon 'real life' scenarios. The questions will often be 'open-ended'.

You must be able to deconstruct the scenario given and then reconstruct the facts, issues and judgements as part of your answer.

Deconstruct

1. Read and consider requirement(s)
2. Read question thoroughly (annotate)
3. Identify key issues:
   - Business
   - Ethical/PCRT
   - Tax
   - Additional information
4. Identify tax principles that address the issues

Reconstruct

5. Start writing
   - Logical order
   - Prioritise key issues
   - Follow the question flow
6. Conclusion
   - Overall issue
   - Added value

Alert! Don't fail to plan or spend too long planning.

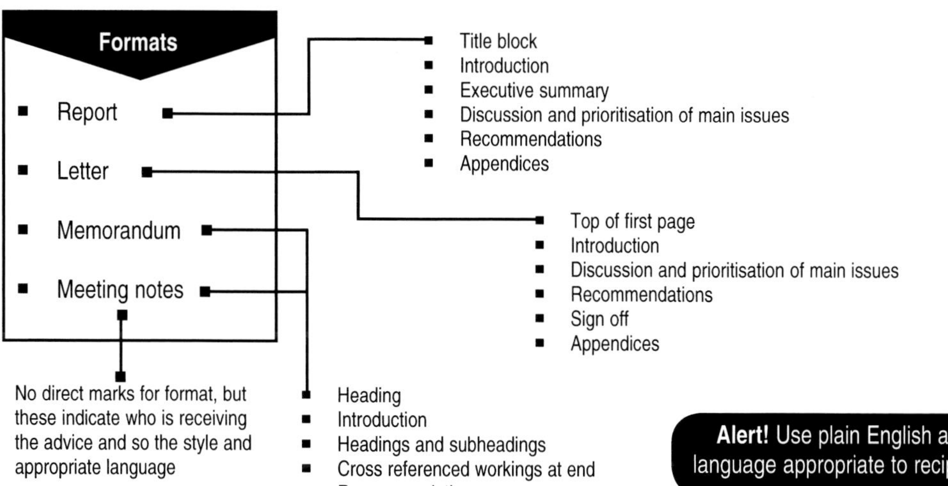

Alert! Use plain English and language appropriate to recipient.

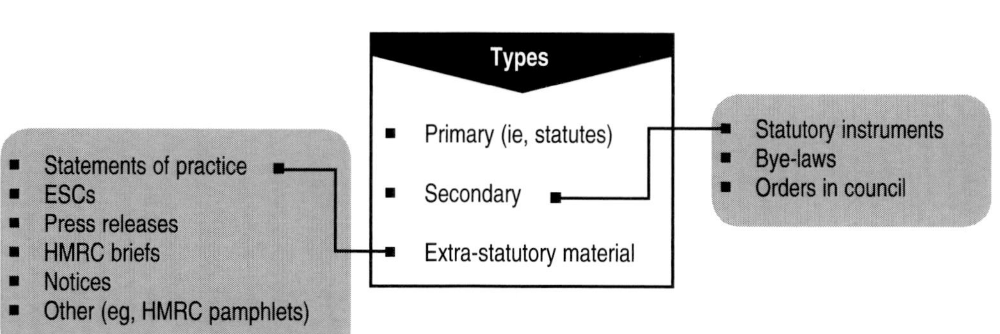
Types
Primary (ie, statutes)
Secondary
Extra-statutory material
Statutory instruments
Bye-laws
Orders in council
Statements of practice
ESCs
Press releases
HMRC briefs
Notices
Other (eg, HMRC pamphlets)

21: Choice of business structure

Topic List

You need to be able to advise on the most appropriate business or corporate structure for a given scenario.

You must also be able to advise on the most tax efficient method of withdrawing profits from a business for a given scenario.

Sole trader

- IT @ max 45%
- NIC max @ 9%/2%
- POAs
  - 31 January in tax year
  - 31 July after tax year
- Balance 31 January after tax year
- CGT on disposal of chargeable assets
- BPR for IHT if transfer whole business

Company

- CT @ 19%
- Extracted profit taxable at IT rates
- NIC for:
  - Employee: max @12%
  - Employer: max @ 13.8%
- Operate PAYE
- CT paid 9m and one day after AP end
- Gains:
  - CT on disposal of chargeable assets
  - Proceeds extracted at IT rates
- BPR for IHT on any number of unquoted trading company shares

Extracting profits from a co

Remuneration

Cash (eg, salary)

- IT @ up to 45%
- NIC @ up to 12%

Benefits

- Exempt = tax free
- Taxable = IT

Employer

- Deductible for CT
- NIC on cash and taxable benefits

Dividends

- Cash/in specie
- First £2,000 0% IT
- IT @ 7.5%/ 32.5%/38.1%
- No NIC
- Not deductible for CT

Pensions

- PPS eg, SIPP
- OPS eg, SSAS

Incentive schemes

- Not tax-advantaged
  - IT and NIC on exercise
- Tax-advantaged
  - Usually no IT/NIC
  - CSOP
  - EMI
  - SAYE
  - SIP

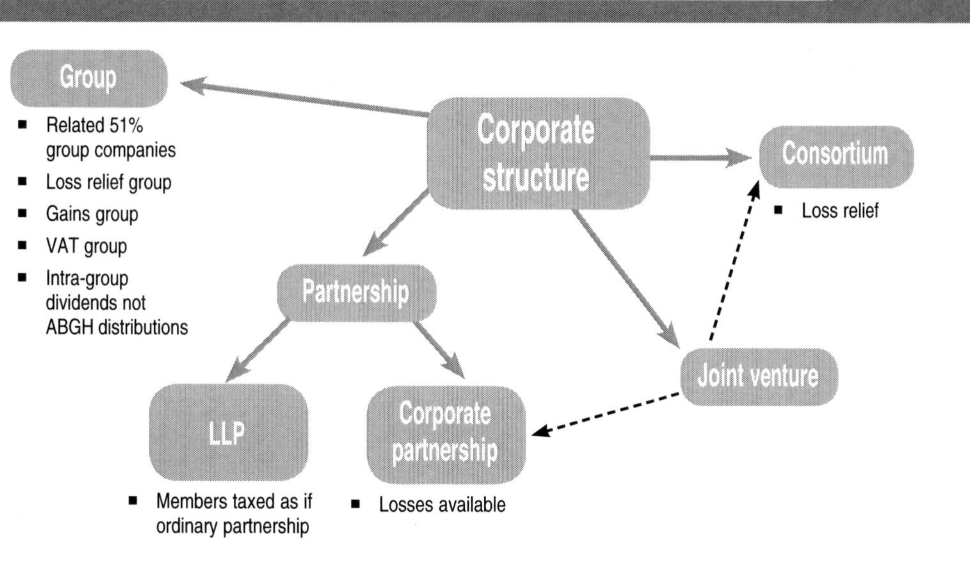
Corporate structure
Group
Related 51% group companies
Loss relief group
Gains group
VAT group
Intra-group dividends not ABGH distributions
Consortium
Loss relief
Partnership
Joint venture
LLP
Members taxed as if ordinary partnership
Corporate partnership
Losses available

22: Leases and property businesses

Topic List

- Leases
- Assignment of leases
- Grant of leases
- Property businesses
- Residential property letting
- Residential property development
- Commercial property

You need to be able to deal with different types of leases that may be disposed of within a property business.

You must be able to advise on the varying tax implications of different types of property business.

Lease premiums

If a lease is granted for 50 years or less for a premium (**P**), the part of the premium taxable as rent on the landlord is:

$$\mathbf{P} \times \frac{50 - \mathbf{Y}}{50}$$

Y = number of years on the lease *minus* 1

↓

If tenant is a trader can divide this amount over length of lease and deduct from trading profits

↓

Adjust if sub-let

Assignment of a lease

Sale of existing interest

- **Long lease: more than 50 years to run**

  Ordinary disposal computation

- **Short lease: 50 years or less to run**

  Write down cost using table of percentages

  ↓

- Allowable cost = $\frac{x}{y}$ × original cost

  % re: number of years to run
  – When assigned = x
  – When acquired = y

- Percentages must be worked out to the nearest month, taking 1/12 of the difference between two adjacent figures in the table for each month

Example

Mr Miggles bought a 30 year lease on 1 June 2017 for £30,000. He assigned it on 1 June 2020 for £70,000. Compute the gain arising.

	£
Disposal proceeds	70,000
Less £30,000 × $\frac{83.816}{87.330}$	(28,793)
	41,207

% (27) = 83.816 % (30) = 87.330

Alert! Tax rates on sale or grant of lease over residential property are 18%/28%

Grant of a lease

Owner/landlord creates a new lease for a tenant to occupy the property.

- **Long lease: grant lease of > 50 years**

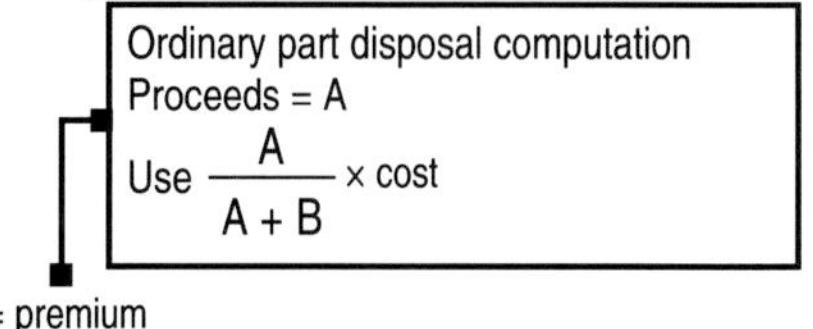

Ordinary part disposal computation

Proceeds = A

Use $\frac{A}{A + B} \times \text{cost}$

A = premium

B = value of remainder (reversionary interest)

- **Short lease: grants lease of ≤ 50 years**

Out of the freehold or original lease > 50 yrs

Modified part disposal computation

Proceeds = a

Use $\frac{a}{A + B} \times \text{cost}$

a = capital element of premium $P \times \frac{(n - 1)}{50}$

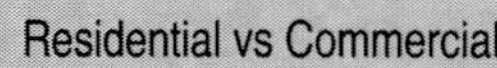

'Flipping' vs letting

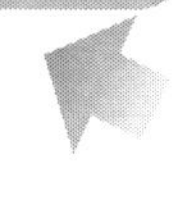

Different types of investment

Property businesses

Choice of business structure

Individual ownership of property

NR companies charged to CT on UK property income

Residential property letting (Buy-to-Let)

	Individual	Company
SDLT	▪ Residential property rates plus additional 3%	▪ Residential property rates plus additional 3% ▪ 15% SDLT if single dwelling > £500,000
ATED	▪ Does not apply	▪ Payable on a dwelling > £500,000
VAT	▪ Purchase/sale of new residential – zero rated ▪ Purchase/sale existing residential – exempt ▪ Most leases – exempt ▪ No OTT on residential property	▪ As for individual
IT/CT	▪ Allowable deduction for domestic items ▪ Restriction on finance costs (Except FHLs) ▪ Rent-a-room (Except FHLs) ▪ accruals basis for receipts over £150k otherwise cash basis ▪ £1,000 property allowance	▪ Accruals basis ▪ Allowable deduction for domestic items ▪ Finance costs are NLTR debits ▪ Taxed at 19%

Except FHLs

	Individual	Company
	■ Taxed at 20%/40% and 45%	■ Extracted profits subject to income tax (salary/dividend)
Losses	■ Pool in a tax year ■ Carry forward against property income	■ Pool in a tax year ■ Relieve property losses against total income in the year, then carry forward against total income ■ NTLR deficits on finance cost can be relieved (see earlier)
Gains	■ CGT at 18%/28	■ CT at 19%
IHT	■ Properties in death estate (no RNRB) ■ No BPR on death	■ Shares in death estate ■ No BPR (investment business)

Except FHLs

Residential property development ('flipping' properties)

Individuals: differences from letting

- No restriction on finance costs
- PPR may be available if it has been used by the individual
- BPR may be available for construction business
- SDLT additional 3% can be avoided in certain limited situations

Company: preferred route?

- No interest relief restriction
- Profits and gains at 19%
- Possible BPR on shares

Commercial property

	Individual	Company
SDLT	■ Non-residential property rates	■ As for individual
VAT	■ Construction/sale of new non-residential standard rated ■ Improving existing commercial – standard rated ■ Sale of older building – exempt ■ Leases – exempt ■ OTT available	■ As for individual
IT/CT	■ Taxed at 20%/40% and 45%	■ Taxed at 19% ■ Extracted profits subject to income tax (salary/dividend)

	Individual	Company
Losses	■ Pool in a tax year ■ Carry forward against property income	■ Pool in a tax year ■ Relieve property losses against total income in the year, then carry forward against total income ■ NLTR deficits on finance cost can be relieved (see earlier)
Gains	■ CGT at 10%/20%	■ CT at 19%
IHT	■ Properties in death estate (no RNRB) ■ Possible BPR on death (property development)	■ Shares in death estate ■ Possible BPR on death (property development)

23: Transformation of owner-managed businesses

Topic List

You must be able to advise on and calculate the tax liabilities arising from the incorporation of an unincorporated business and the disincorporation of a company.

You must also be able to advise on and calculate the tax liabilities arising from the bankruptcy of an individual.

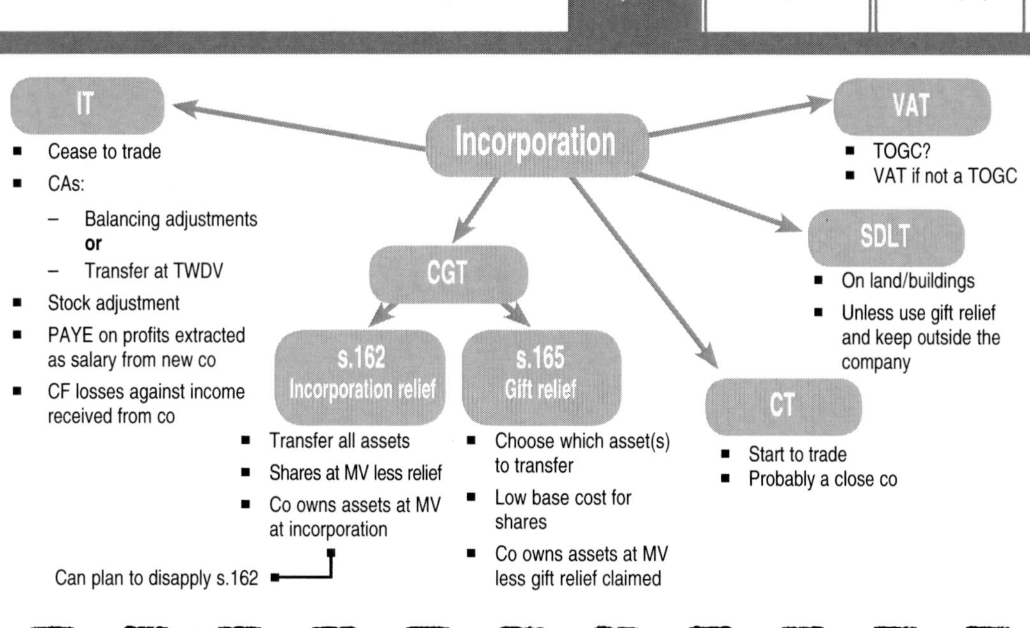

Incorporation
IT
Cease to trade
CAs:
– Balancing adjustments
or
– Transfer at TWDV
Stock adjustment
PAYE on profits extracted as salary from new co
CF losses against income received from co
CGT
s.162
Incorporation relief
Transfer all assets
Shares at MV less relief
Co owns assets at MV at incorporation
Can plan to disapply s.162
s.165
Gift relief
Choose which asset(s) to transfer
Low base cost for shares
Co owns assets at MV less gift relief claimed
CT
Start to trade
Probably a close co
VAT
TOGC?
VAT if not a TOGC
SDLT
On land/buildings
Unless use gift relief and keep outside the company

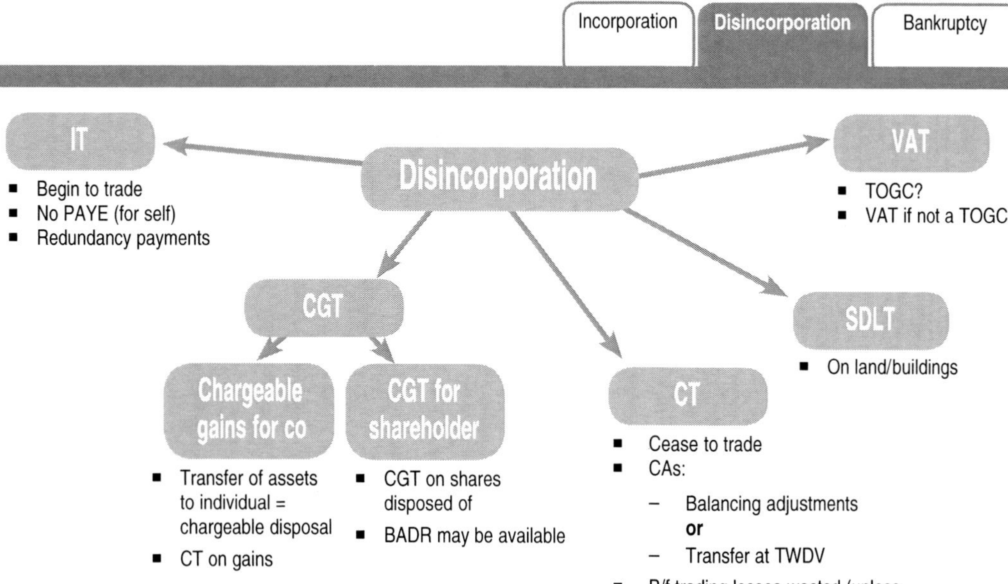

IT

- Begin to trade
- No PAYE (for self)
- Redundancy payments

VAT

- TOGC?
- VAT if not a TOGC

SDLT

- On land/buildings

Chargeable gains for co

- Transfer of assets to individual = chargeable disposal
- CT on gains

CGT for shareholder

- CGT on shares disposed of
- BADR may be available

CT

- Cease to trade
- CAs:
  - Balancing adjustments

    or
  - Transfer at TWDV
- B/f trading losses wasted (unless terminal loss relief available)

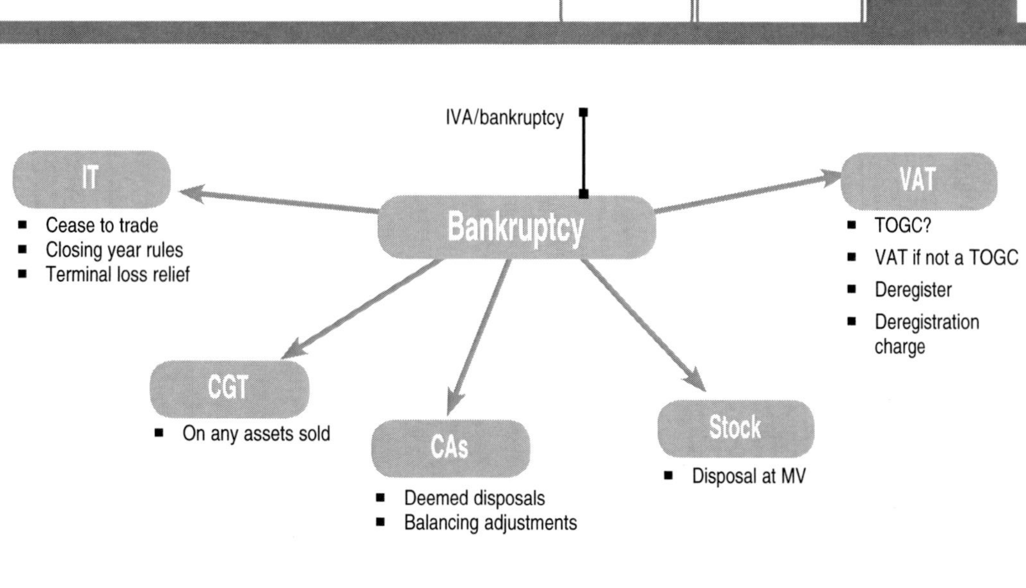
IVA/bankruptcy
Bankruptcy
IT
Cease to trade
Closing year rules
Terminal loss relief
CGT
On any assets sold
CAs
Deemed disposals
Balancing adjustments
Stock
Disposal at MV
VAT
TOGC?
VAT if not a TOGC
Deregister
Deregistration charge

24: Corporate reorganisations

Topic List

You must be able to advise on, and calculate the tax liabilities arising from, the disposal of a corporate business, the transfer of a trade within a group and the hive down of a trade.

You must also be able to advise on and explain the tax implications of a management buy out.

Sale of shares vs sale of assets

Sale of shares	Sale of assets
Shareholder selling shares	**Company selling assets**
Capital gain/loss	Capital gain/loss on disposals
B/f capital losses reduce gain	IFA disposals = taxable credits/allowable debits
Reduce gain by pre-sale dividend	■ Balancing adjustments for CAs ■ Unless elect to transfer at TWDV
Defer gain if share for share (paper for paper)	Rollover relief may be available
	■ If sells trade, will cease to trade ■ AP ends ■ Trading losses lost
SD at 0.5% by purchaser of shares	SDLT at up to 5% by purchaser of land and buildings (assuming non-residential)
Exempt share sale for VAT	■ VAT payable unless TOGC ■ Property may still be subject to VAT ■ Usage adjustment for CGS assets

Sale of shares vs sale of assets

Sale of shares	Sale of assets
Corporate shareholders	**Corporate shareholders of company**
SSE may apply to gain	■ Extract after-tax proceeds as dividend ■ Usually exempt ■ May be an ABGH distribution
Group implications: ■ Reduction in related 51% group companies ■ Loss of group relief ■ Degrouping charge for gains	
Individual shareholders	**Individual shareholders of company**
Reliefs for gains: ■ EIS/SEIS ■ BADR	■ Take funds as income (dividend) or capital (if part of liquidation) ■ Tax on these funds = double tax charge

Advantages of share deal

Vendor

- No double tax charge – only tax gain on shares
- SSE available
- AP does not end
- No CA balancing adjustments

Purchaser

- Losses of target company available
- Stamp duty at 0.5%
- Legally straightforward as contracts pass with co

Disadvantages of share deal

Vendor

- Degrouping charge

Purchaser

- Assets acquired at TWDV
- Contingent liabilities pass to co

Advantages of asset deal

Vendor

- Rollover relief may be available

Purchaser

- MV usually > TWDV
- May create tax-deductible goodwill
- Roll gains over into new assets
- Uplift to MV for assets
- Legal liabilities remain with vendor

Disadvantages of asset deal

Vendor

- CA balancing charge may arise
- Possible further gain on liquidation

Purchaser

- Losses remain with vendor
- SDLT @ up to 5% on land and buildings (assuming non-residential)
- Irrecoverable VAT may arise
- Must transfer contracts so legally = more complex

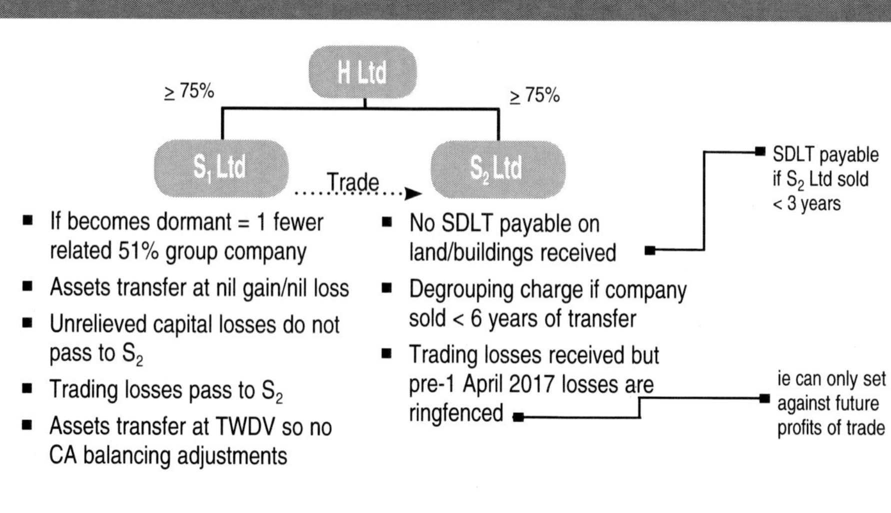
H Ltd
≥ 75%
≥ 75%
S1 Ltd
Trade
S2 Ltd
If becomes dormant = 1 fewer related 51% group company
Assets transfer at nil gain/nil loss
Unrelieved capital losses do not pass to S2
Trading losses pass to S2
Assets transfer at TWDV so no CA balancing adjustments
No SDLT payable on land/buildings received
SDLT payable if S2 Ltd sold < 3 years
Degrouping charge if company sold < 6 years of transfer
Trading losses received but pre-1 April 2017 losses are ringfenced
ie can only set against future profits of trade

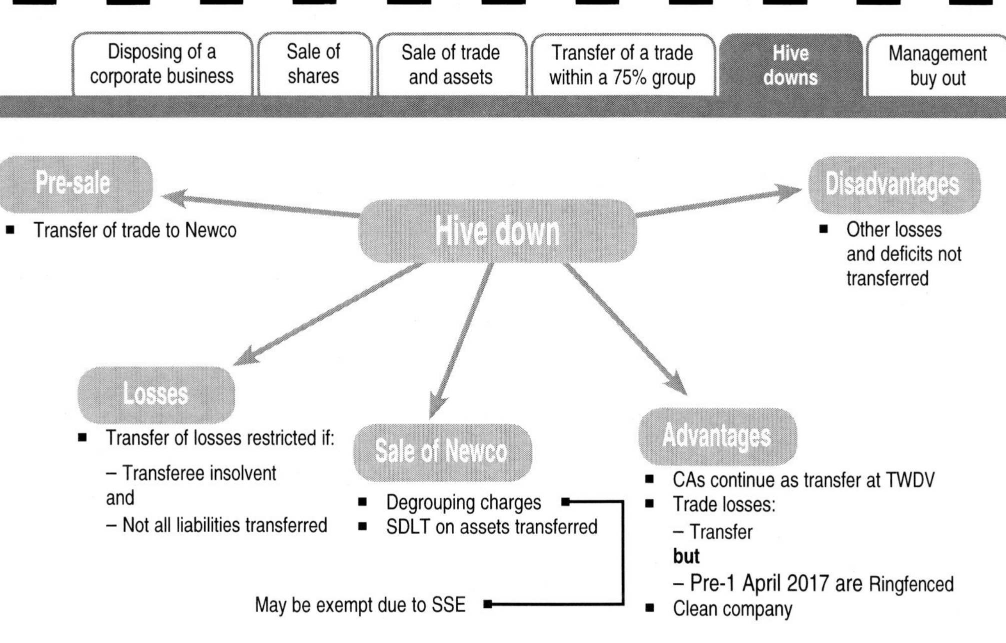
Hive down
Pre-sale
Transfer of trade to Newco
Disadvantages
Other losses and deficits not transferred
Losses
Transfer of losses restricted if:
– Transferee insolvent
and
– Not all liabilities transferred
Sale of Newco
Degrouping charges
SDLT on assets transferred
May be exempt due to SSE
Advantages
CAs continue as transfer at TWDV
Trade losses:
– Transfer
but
– Pre-1 April 2017 are Ringfenced
Clean company

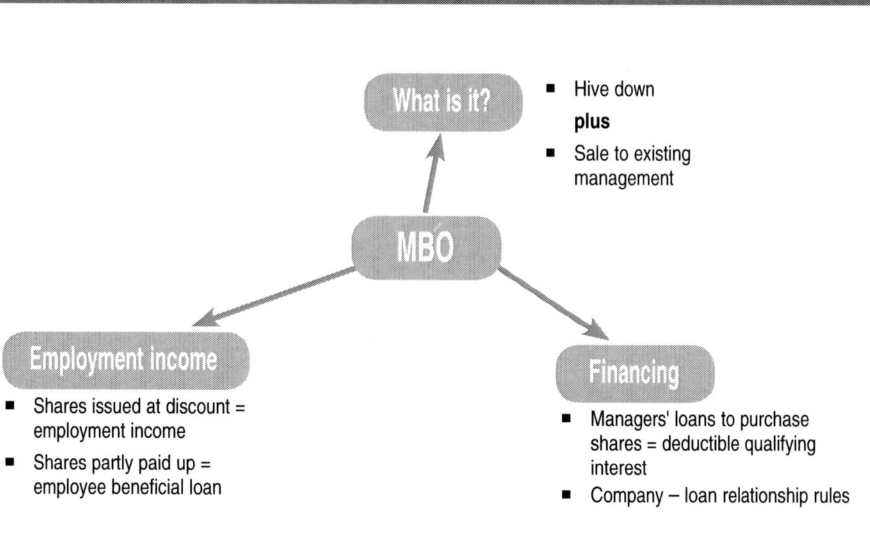
MBO
What is it?
■ Hive down
plus
■ Sale to existing management
Employment income
■ Shares issued at discount = employment income
■ Shares partly paid up = employee beneficial loan
Financing
■ Managers' loans to purchase shares = deductible qualifying interest
■ Company – loan relationship rules

Notes

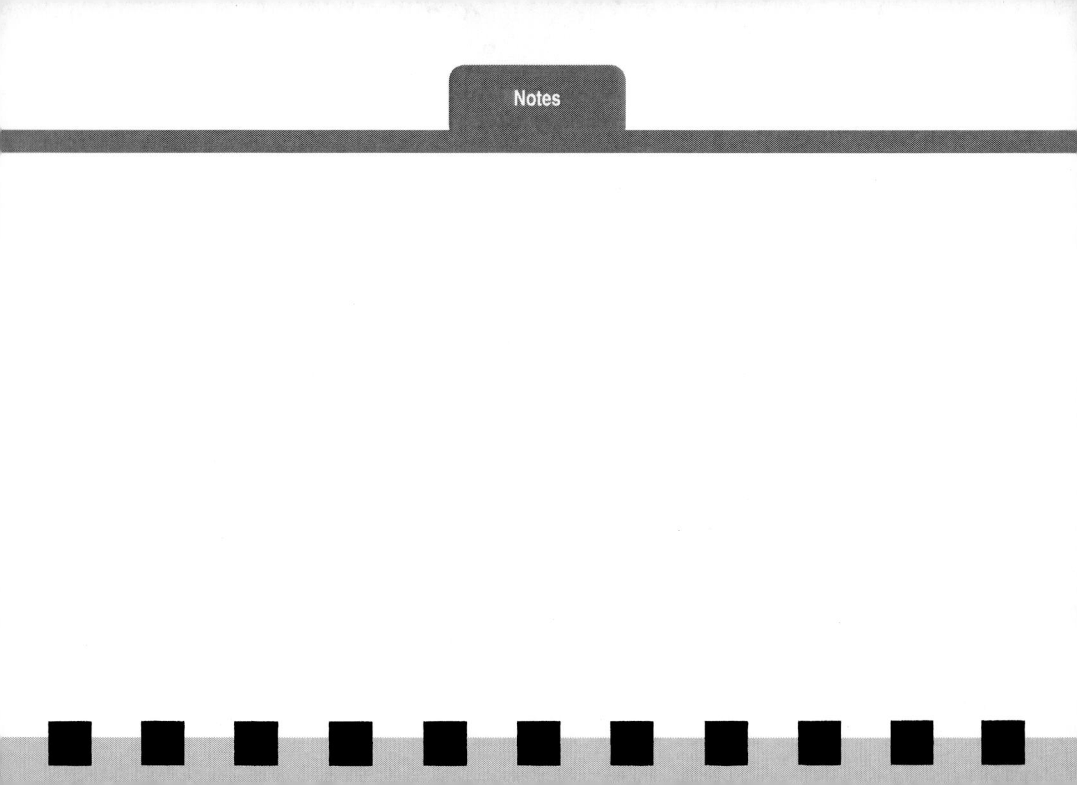

Notes

Notes

Notes